ESSENTIAL EFFECTS
Water, Fire, Wind, and More

ESSENTIAL EFFECTS
Water, Fire, Wind, and More

by

MAURO MARESSA

CRC Press
Taylor & Francis Group
Boca Raton London New York

CRC Press is an imprint of the
Taylor & Francis Group, an **informa** business

A FOCAL PRESS BOOK

CRC Press
Taylor & Francis Group
6000 Broken Sound Parkway NW, Suite 300
Boca Raton, FL 33487-2742

© 2018 by Taylor & Francis Group, LLC
CRC Press is an imprint of Taylor & Francis Group, an Informa business

No claim to original U.S. Government works

Printed on acid-free paper

International Standard Book Number-13: 978-1-138-10107-4 (Paperback)
978-1-138-19692-6 (Hardback)

Library of Congress Cataloging-in-Publication Data

Names: Maressa, Mauro, author.
Title: Essential effects : water, fire, wind, and more / Mauro Maressa.
Description: Boca Raton : Taylor & Francis, a CRC title, part of the Taylor & Francis
imprint, a member of the Taylor & Francis Group, the academic
division of T&F Informa, plc, [2017]
Identifiers: LCCN 2017004029| ISBN 9781138196926 (hardback : alk. paper) |
ISBN 9781138101074 (pbk. : alk. paper)
Subjects: LCSH: Computer animation. | Physical geography--Computer
simulation. | Cinematography--Special effects.
Classification: LCC TR897.7 .M3747 2017 | DDC 777/.7--dc23
LC record available at https://lccn.loc.gov/2017004029

Visit the Taylor & Francis Web site at
http://www.taylorandfrancis.com

and the CRC Press Web site at
http://www.crcpress.com

Printed and bound in the United States of America by Sheridan

For my family,
without whose love and support
none of this would have been
possible, especially Cindy!

Contents

Foreword

I am very honored to have been asked to write this foreword to Mauro's book on traditional effects in animation. I was fortunate to have had Mauro come to work with me at my studio back in the late eighties and early nineties. He added class to the commercials we produced and raised the quality level above most commercials being done back then. I was always thrilled at what he added to our work. When you read about the golden age of animation, when they started taking effects animation seriously, making it a special department at the Disney studio, you realize that the research that went into the development of the different effects was astounding. Mauro would think and attack individual problems on a project with the same attention to detail, and his work showed it.

Personally, I've always been in awe of animated effects, probably because I have no idea how they do it. I'm a character animator by trade and I'm always amazed that when an animated film does well, it's the lead character animators who are interviewed about their part in the film. Being a character animator, you'd think I'd be okay with that. But throughout my entire career I have admired everyone behind the scenes, all the unsung heroes of these films. If it wasn't for the visual development people, the layout people, the voice talent, and so many others, I wouldn't have had a stage to perform on or a voice to inspire me. But it's the effects animators who create the surrounding elements of the world of the film and bring it to life. Traditional effects animators don't copy reality, as is often the case with computer animation today; they capture the essence of what we feel when we see water or flames or smoke. They create effects as a design that audiences accept readily, an impression of these elements. Effects, sometimes, become characters themselves.

Frank Thomas and Ollie Johnston expressed this quite well in their book *The Illusion of Life* when they said, "The Effects Animator is a special kind of artist: he has a curiosity about the way things work, a feel for the mechanical, and usually sees great beauty in the patterns of nature … creating spirit in the movement of water and lava, drama in fires and storms, and astonishing loveliness in the handling of falling leaves and snow." In the hands of someone like Mauro, when the characters of Pacha and Kuzco fall into the water in *The Emperor's New Groove*, as stylized as the water is, you feel wet. Their work feels seamless; it doesn't jump out at you as the main feature of the scene but enhances it. Effects animators like Mauro know when it should be in the background, or when it should be the main focus but always supporting the scene, so that we tend to take their work for granted, as perhaps we should.

In CG animation, we are able to create effects that seem more real than reality, making it very well suited for a live-action movie. Unfortunately, CG effects often do not relate well to the character animation. By contrast, in traditionally animated films everything fits like a glove, a perfect design. At my studio, I was so fortunate to have talented people, the right people, and one of them was Mauro. When you look at Mauro's accomplishments in this business and in art in general, it's impressive: from teaching his craft to being an effects animator as well as a character animator, both in traditional 2D and his work with computer animation in live-action films, as well as being an incredible sculptor. It's a body of work that reflects Mauro's love of art and it shows in everything he does. Plus he's a joy to work with.

With all of the books on animation that have been written over the years, I'm surprised that there hasn't been more done solely on effects animation, so all I can say is, "It's about time!" But this book was well worth waiting for, because it is literally a gift from one of the industry's most talented artists. Study it well and help continue an incredible legacy of animated effects, started by some of the legendary effects animators in the business.

Dale Baer
Disney Animation
Supervising Animator

Preface

As a traditional effects animator, in order to animate, I need to use all the resources available to me. I draw with my right hand, which I call the *artist*. I use my left, which I call the *technology*, to flip and roll my animation drawings. If I use only my right hand, it may result in a nice drawing and potentially a great standalone piece of art. If I only use my left hand to flip the drawing I will end up with a very wrinkled piece of paper. The brain is in the middle to reason out timing, volumes, composition, arcs, action, design, and so on. In order for me to animate properly, I need all the resources available to me to work in unison. While my hands do the physical work, it is my mind that needs to recall the stored information that I have accumulated through study and observation. Without that stored information, you are going to be stumbling along hoping you're going in the right direction. The rolling of the animation drawings is my playback machine, which allows me to view the action of my animation four to five drawings at a time. Today's technology allows us to animate in a computer, but we are missing the direct physical connection with the drawing. That tangible association is what I miss most. The network that is the brain to hand to paper, the direct current of creating a piece of animation from my mind through my hand to the paper, is a joy I can't imagine not experiencing. That's why I think the use of a stylus on a tablet is more palpable to me. While the computer is an incredible tool, I have to use a number of commands for it to do what I want it to do, and then I may have to go to another program and another set of commands to continue to create my animation. I guess I just don't have the mindset. I envy how some people can use the computer and their amazing accomplishments. It's a tool that I would encourage every artist to learn how to use. But remember that the tool does not dictate the art! It is the artist who must incorporate his tools with his art, be they a pencil or a computer.

What I hope to impart to you in this book is a series of basics lessons and examples on which you can build a foundation for animating effects. These are techniques that a tech-savvy animator can also use and really should know and use in his or her animation. When I'm teaching, I try to get my students to understand that in order to build a strong foundation for a career in effects animation, you must pay attention to basics. You want a strong foundation when you build a house so that it will stand for a long time. You don't want to build a career that flounders and collapses. Too often I've seen young animators who want to step in and animate the most complex of scenes and who get frustrated when they have to do things over and over again without reaching the desired results simply because their process and techniques fall short from lack of a basic understanding of how things work or physical theory. While I can admire their desire and passion to jump in and attack a challenge, I can't help but shake my head at their unwillingness to work at learning all they need to, so that they can attempt to combine all the little intricacies that make up the more elaborate and complex ones.

There is a certain poetry of sorts in animating effects. The ebb and flow of a design within the context of an environment created in a film. The way water flows and smoke rises to the sky or is specifically designed for that environment that lets the viewers accept the veracity of the scene without hitting them over the head with the effects. I have often said to people who want to know what I did in a film, "If I do my job right you will never notice what I did, but if I muck it up, it may take the viewer out of the picture and disturb the flow of the storyline!"

An effects animator's job is not to lead the storytelling but to accompany it and help the story move forward. An effect may frame the mood of the character or his or her surroundings (see Figure P.1).

FIG P.1 Disney's *Beauty and the Beast*: firelight.

At times the effect may make a statement to emphasize a climactic moment (see Figure P.2).

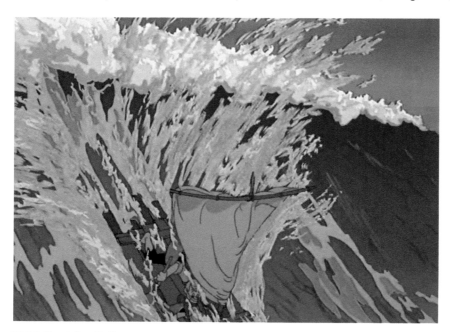

FIG P.2 Disney's *Pinocchio*: Monstro ocean wave.

More often than not, the effects are a minor character, often playing a minor role, that accompanies the characters through their journey in the film. It is a specialized field within the specialized media of animation. It has been an incredible experience for me that has been both gratifying and rewarding in more ways than I can say. Animation has been a joy for me. I would jump out of bed every morning eager to start my day. Imagine, they paid me a salary to draw all day and make a living doing it and to work with some of the most interesting and talented people I have ever known! Don't get me wrong, it's a lot of hard work and can be grueling and repetitive at times, but it has also been greatly satisfying and worth the hard work. I'll wager that anyone you ask about their animation careers will say the same thing. It has been a tremendous journey that I don't foresee ending for me any time soon in the future. All that I have learned along the way has and will still help me in whatever new challenges I may encounter in my later years. I'm certain you will feel the same way about it.

Introduction

I was born in Italy and moved to the United States with my family in 1959. My father preceded my mother and the three children by 3 years, establishing himself before having the rest of us come join him. We moved to Milford, Massachusetts, where my brother and sister and I grew up. My father worked as a tailor for a couple of different companies, while my mother worked as a seamstress. After a few years, they had saved enough to buy a house with a storefront, from which they operated their tailor shop until their retirement in the late 1980s. My brother showed promise as a fashion designer, and after attending school in Boston and New York became successful in that profession until his sudden and untimely death in 1999. My younger sister attended college and later on would marry and have two children. After high school, I went to art school and studied fine arts at the New England School of Art in Boston and then went on to the University of Massachusetts at Amherst to get my BFA.

I started teaching art in the Milford school system that year. It was the same year I would meet my future wife, Cynthia. We got married 2 years later and decided that, since I had the summers off from teaching, it would be great to take a cross-country trip for our honeymoon. So we drove through 36 states in our van. Along the way, as we drove through Los Angeles, because I was a big fan of Disney I decided to try my luck at the studio in Burbank. I didn't think anything of it at that time, but something like that is not possible today. I parked on the street across from the main entrance and walked to the security offices, where I asked if I could get an interview for the animation department. The nice lady instructed me to have a seat, and 20 minutes later I was interviewed by a nice gray-haired man who looked at my portfolio and was very positive. Knowing that I lived in Massachusetts, he told me that if I ever decided to move to Los Angeles I should try the studio again. When I got back to the van and Cindy waiting patiently inside, I told her about the interview and discussed the possibility of moving to Los Angeles for the rest of the trip home. We moved to Los Angeles 6 months later!

We got settled in and Cindy was able to find work at a department store. It was a bit of luck that Cindy happened to mention to one of her coworker friends that I was applying for work at Disney. Her friend, Betty, was an older lady who happened to have a friend that worked at Disney and asked if I would like to meet him. She invited us to a dinner party at her house about a week later where I met Donald "Don" Duckwall. He was a very gracious man and asked me if I would like to have a tour at the studio and to be sure to bring my portfolio with me. I met with Don the following week at the studio, and he gave me a tour of the animation building on the main lot. One of the people he introduced me to on the tour was Eric Larson. Eric was one of Walt Disney's "Nine Old Men" and was head of the training program there. I had never met a nicer, gentler, and more unassuming man in all my life. He looked at my portfolio and made some comments about the work but said that after 6 months in animation I would probably see a marked improvement in my drawings and how I posed my characters. He asked whether I would like to enter the animation training program. I had no idea what I was doing and only had an inkling of how animation was produced, but I loved the films and wanted to be involved in the making of them. Of course I jumped at the opportunity and started studying under Eric's patient tutelage in April. My two animation tests went well, but I fell victim to layoff due to the end of production on "The Small One," a short film done by Don Bluth at the studio at the time. There was no need to keep a newcomer like me while they were gearing up on their next film, especially when they had experienced artists already! I soon learned that layoffs are a common occurrence in the animation industry and animators would just pick up and move on to the next job.

Don Duckwall came in to tell me the news and informed me that he had called Harry Love, who was looking for artists at Hanna-Barbera.

So I went to work at Hanna-Barbera and was there for the next 3 years. I started out as an assistant animator, and my job would be to follow up on the work of the seasoned animators working on such Saturday morning cartoons as *Godzilla*, *SuperFriends*, *Fred and Barney*, *The Smurfs*, and *Scooby-Doo and Scrappy-Doo*. It was an incredible learning experience for me and indeed for all of us young animators who were in the early stages of our careers and soon to go on to be a part of the renaissance of traditional animation of the late 1980s throughout the 1990s! We all worked under the mentorship of animators who had started their careers in the 1930s and were still going strong, animators like Irv Spence, Hal Ambro, Volus Jones, Ken Muse, Ed Barge, Dave Tendlar, Ed Aardal, Oliver "Lefty" Callahan, Charlie Downs, Rudi Cataldi, and so many others. They were animators who all started working at such studios as MGM, Disney, Fleischer, and UPA, and all had notable careers. My immediate supervisors were Bill Kile and Bob Goe. After settling in at Hanna-Barbera, I kept going to Bill and Bob for test animation assignments that I could work on at home in the evenings, which they would then look at and critique. I had set up a rig on my drawing desk at home with a hole cut in the center and a piece of Plexiglas with floating pegs for my animation paper. I did this for the next 6–7 months almost every night, working on animation of people and animal characters from the shows we were working on at the studio that Bill or Bob would make up for me until Bill surprised me one day and gave me a production scene to work on. It was on *SuperFriends* and it was a character riding a metal horse crossing railroad tracks and getting stuck in the tracks. After that Bill would give me a scene to work on regularly until he promoted me to animator (see Figure I.1).

FIG I.1 Me as an apprentice animator at Hanna-Barbera, 1979. Photo by Lyn J. Kroeger.

Hanna-Barbera began working on an animation feature called *Heidi's Song*, and Bob Taylor would be the director. Bob gave me the opportunity to come work on that feature, and I worked closely under Hal Ambro, Irv Spence, and Charlie Downs as well as regularly talking with other people, whom I was constantly asking for pointers. All the animators at the studio animated their characters as well as any effects that might be part of those scenes.

Bob Taylor directed me to Ed Aardal one day when I got a scene that had a lot of effects in it. Ed was an old-time animator who started working as a character and effects animator at Disney in 1939. Ed was a great and patient teacher and spent many hours teaching me about effects. I suddenly started excelling at doing effects. So I got to work on a lot more scenes that had both characters and effects! Charlie Downs broke his wrists while roller skating one day and was not able to work for a while. He recommended that I take over working on some of his scenes of the Man Mountain character in the film and was given a great opportunity (see Figure I.2).

FIG I.2 Nightmare Mountain from the dream sequence in *Heidi's Song*.

While we were working on *Heidi's Song* at Hanna-Barbera, I picked up freelance work from *Heavy Metal: The Movie*. I was part of the L.A. crew that worked on the "Taarna" sequence of that picture in 1980. After completing *Heidi's Song*, we started on preproduction work for another feature at Hanna-Barbera, but in 1981 I got the opportunity to go to work for Ralph Bakshi on his feature *Fire and Ice*. The idea of working alongside with Frank Frazetta was a chance I could not pass up, so I left Hanna-Barbera. I worked on many of the characters in *Fire and Ice*, but the last 2 weeks of that project had me working on the destruction of Nekron's fortress and the lava sequence. I animated all the lava by using grease pencil on clear celluloid sheets in order to expedite the process, avoiding the Xerox process and going to ink and paint directly, where all they had to do was paint the cels (see Figure I.3).

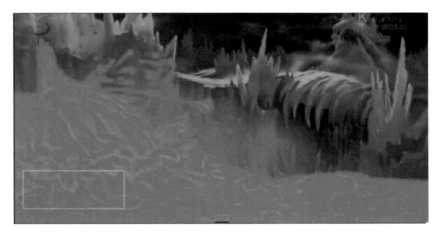

FIG I.3 Bakshi's *Fire and Ice*: lava pouring down a chasm.

After *Fire and Ice*, I returned to Disney as an effects animator on the Tokyo Disneyland pavilion called "Meet the World" and later went on to *The Black Cauldron* as an assistant character animator where I got to work alongside my old pal from Hanna-Barbera, Charlie Downs, once again working on a lot of henchmen and incidental characters.

I chose to leave Disney after that film in 1985 to start a new phase in my career, that of working in live-action special effects. While Boss Film Corp. was gearing up for their next film, *Poltergeist II*, I spent a few months at Filmation Studios in the interim working on *He-Man*, *She-Ra: Princess of Power*, and *Pinocchio and the Emperor of the Night*. Then I started working at Boss, which was a live-action special effects studio headed up by multi-Oscar-winning special effects wizard Richard Edlund, ASC. I worked off and on for Boss over the next 8 years on a number of films: *Poltergeist II*, *The Monster Squad*, *Big Trouble in Little China*, and *Solarbabies* and as animation supervisor for *Far and Away*, *Solar Crisis*, *Batman Returns*, and *Alien 3*. In that same period of time, I also worked at another live-action effects house called *Perpetual Motion Picture* with Barry Nolan on *Bill and Ted's Excellent Adventure* and served as animation supervisor on *Warlock* then as well.

I returned to traditional animation in 1992 at Baer Animation Studios, working with animator Dale Baer and his small group of hard-working and talented artists. We worked on a number of commercials and Disney's *The Prince and the Pauper*, which was outsourced to Baer Studios at the time. I then returned to Disney again in February of 1993 to start animating effects on *Pocahontas*. As that film was not yet ready for a full crew, I was put on the "B" picture called *The Lion King*. Everyone was anxious to work on *Pocahontas* at the time, as that was supposed to be the next blockbuster. No one thought that *The Lion King* would amount to much since it was about a bunch of cute animal characters and would not appeal to many people! 6 or 7 months into production, the crew was invited into the screening room to see the trailer that would be released soon to advertise *The Lion King*. That was the opening sequence of the film! Needless to say, everyone walked out of that screening room 20 minutes later with a renewed sense of energy that lifted the spirits of the entire studio. We all knew we had a hit on our hands! *The Lion King* was a great success and that creative energy carried over to *Pocahontas* and *The Hunchback of Notre Dame*. Even though these films would not be as successful as *The Lion King*, the quality and the artistry on all the films that followed was magnificent! The artists excelled at every level of production.

At this time, Disney Feature Animation was riding a wave of hits, so the studio built a brand-new facility for the Animation Department that would be located next to the main studio in Burbank. A few of us in the Effects Department were some of the first to move into the new building. This was around the time we were working on *The Hunchback of Notre Dame*. The studio had two other feature animation units as well as the Burbank main studio. One was in Orlando, Florida, and one in Paris, France. I was fortunate to get the opportunity to visit each of these studios over a 1 year period to help in the training of the effects departments in each of those studios. They needed very little training, as the artists in both studios were very good.

Both would play an integral part in the production of the LA-based studio productions, and the Florida studio would soon produce two great films of their own: *Lilo and Stitch* and *Brother Bear*. While in Paris, I was asked to join a group of artists from LA on a quick recruiting tour in London and Dublin led by Roy E. Disney. Roy was a true friend and champion of the Animation Department and the main reason animation at the studio survived after Michael Eisner and company came to power at the studio in 1985. At that time, there was serious talk of dismantling the Feature Animation Department, but Roy would have none of that and fought to keep it a viable entity at Disney. He was to be rewarded by seeing the great success that feature animation would have in the 1980s through the 1990s and into the twenty-first century. But the artists were moved from the original animation building that Walt had built and made so many great films in. So, Animation was moved, lock, stock, and barrel, to some warehouses in Glendale a few miles away from the main studio. And it then produced some of the most memorable modern-day animated film classics!

I was in my hotel room in London one evening getting ready to return to Paris and then a week later to return to LA. I received a phone call from Alice Dewey, the producer of the next film scheduled to be released after *Pocahontas*, called *Hercules*, which Ron Clemens and John Musker were to direct after the great success of their last film, *Aladdin*. Alice asked if I would be interested in heading up the Effects Department on that film. I gave it a great deal of thought and pondered all the possibilities of such a task that would be awaiting me and after an intense 2 seconds, I said yes!

I began work on *Hercules* as soon as I returned to the studio in Burbank. There was already a group of effects animators working on designs for the film. So it wasn't long before the art director and directors picked the look they liked for the effects on the film. With the complexity of the design of the water, smoke, fire, and the sheer volume of the number of effects that needed to be done, we needed help from our friends and colleagues in scene planning to fashion techniques to alleviate some of the pressure. *Hercules* was an extremely heavy-effects movie. We not only had a large crew in the Burbank studio but the effects departments in Florida and Paris were also helping us as well. This was true for the other departments on the film, and credit must be given to the coordinated efforts of all the people whose job was to keep track of the hundreds of scenes and thousands of animation drawings. Throughout the production, I found myself repeating, "We're going to need a bigger boat!" Such was the volume of work pouring into the department. But I had a great team of animators and assistants that made it all look easy!

I would be remiss if I didn't mention one of the key animators on my crew, Dorse Lanpher. Dorse was a calming element within the vortex of that production and a great sounding board for me. He had started his animation career in the 1950s at Disney and had experienced and seen just about all there was to see. I was very fortunate to have him as one of my animators and a friend. His astuteness and advice helped me through some rough times in dealing with personalities and the rigors of production. I will be eternally grateful to him. Sadly Dorse passed away in his home in 2011, several years after his retirement, leaving a great many of us that had worked alongside him very sad. He was a mentor to many of us who worked with him and has been sorely missed by us all.

Another key member in the Effects Department was our assistant production manager, Kim Gray. She was an incredibly efficient manager and a great cheerleader who kept things constantly moving forward. The fact that we had crews working in three different time zones, on two continents, and it all fell neatly into place every week was due to the collaborative efforts of a lot of people, and it was good to know you could always depend on everyone knowing their job and carrying it out efficiently. I'm very proud of the people I worked with on my crew and what a great job they all did on a film I am extremely proud of! In 1997, I was honored to receive an Annie Award from ASIFA for my work on *Hercules* and it would not have been possible without the concerted effort of that marvelous crew I had the pleasure of working with!

My next film was to be called *Kingdom of the Sun*—this would eventually become *The Emperor's New Groove* after several rewrites. The artistic leads were sent to research the Inca-based story line. We spent 2 weeks traveling around Peru taking in as much of the culture as possible, then returned to LA and started on the production. The original story was going to be much more ambitious. The original concept of the director, Roger Allers (*The Lion King*), was a bit darker and more mystical story with plenty of special effects. The story went through a rewrite (a common occurrence in the animation world) and a change of leadership. It's a story documented in a film called *Sweatbox*, done by Trudie Styler, wife of the singer–songwriter Sting who was doing the music for *Kingdom*. The effects crew ended up being considerably smaller than originally thought.

While we all waited for the story changes, our crew ended up being loaned out to other projects in the works. I, along with a small group of animators and assistants, worked on the sequence of *Fantasia 2000* called "Rhapsody in Blue" directed by Eric Goldberg (*Pocahontas*). This was a very simple and highly stylized-looking film with the clean line look of Al Hirschfeld, the great caricaturist of Broadway stars and many other celebrities. When we finally got back on our film, it was now called *The Emperor's New Groove* and was more of a comedy. Under the new Director, Mark Dindal (*Cats Don't Dance*), the production went into high gear and was finished in time to meet the scheduled release date that had been set for the original *Kingdom* film—a tribute to Mark's leadership.

My first foray into digitally animated features was *Chicken Little*, again working with Mark Dindal. I started out designing the effects and then later animating effects. I mostly animated cars and spaceships in Maya® for that film. My effects designs were for reference for the digital animators and programmers to try and emulate the digital effects into the more cartoony look the director wanted for the film, which they did quite successfully. The second digitally animated film I worked on was *Meet the Robinsons* and on this film my role was purely as an animator, mostly props and vehicles and a bit of elemental effects (and bubbles).

Around this time, it was clear that the studio was going 100% digital. Although there had been massive layoffs a few years before after the traditionally animated feature *Home on the Range* in 2004, a great many more were laid off in 2007, and I was one of them. I returned about 9 months later to work on what would be the last two-dimensional traditionally animated feature that Disney would do to this date, *The Princess and the Frog*. The great part of working on *Princess* was that we worked on Cintiq® tablets with styluses and produced our effects on the tablets. We were able to do our own manipulation of the effects using the Toon Boom Harmony program, so that we were able to hand over a nearly finished effects element to color model. The art director could then make his final tweaks with a minimum of effort as the basics of the elements were already blocked out, allowing the art director to concentrate on the fine-tuning of the effects to his liking.

I now teach traditional character animation and effects animation at Otis College of Art and Design in Los Angeles and do some work on independently produced traditional animated films, TV shows, and commercials, as well as my personal artwork.

CHAPTER 1

A History of Effects in Animation

I only went out for a walk and finally concluded to stay out till sundown,
for going out, I found, I was really going in.

—*John Muir*

Early on in animation, the animators did all their own effects as well as the character animation that may have been called for in the scenes they were working on. Often, the effects were more or less an afterthought to the gags the characters were acting out. Therefore the effects were usually haphazard and simplistic interpretations of the particular effect. Water was a flat mass with possibly some lines in it to indicate a directional flow that broke up like bits of torn paper when it hit a character. Smoke was a cycle of round shapes rising upward or covering the screen, the simplest and most elementary of designs. This was not a slight on the part of character animators. During the silent era, animators were cranking out one film per week. This left very little time for study or experimentation for improving the quality of effects in those shorts. The effects were done simply to convey the idea of fire, or water, or smoke, or whatever the gag called for, and the effect was usually on the same level as the characters, so there was very little chance of utilizing any camera effects, like diffusion or opacity.

Some of the very first drawn animation that I have found was on short films done by J. Stuart Blackton, considered by some to be the father of American animation. Blackton was producing animated sequences as early as 1900. These films were distributed by the Edison Studios. *Humorous Phases of Funny Faces* was released in 1906. Blackton used chalk on a blackboard smudged to make smoke "effects," the earliest hand-drawn "animated effect" on film that I have found (see Figure 1.1).

FIG 1.1 J. Stuart Blackton's *Humorous Phases of Funny Faces.*

Another early pioneer was Emile Cohl, who in 1908 produced *Fantasmagorie*, which had stick figures morphing into other figures. This has been credited as the first fully animated film. Camera effects started getting more creative (see Figure 1.2).

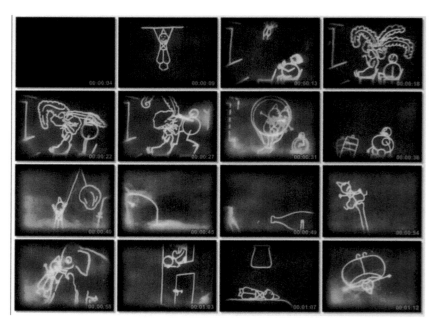

FIG 1.2 Emile Cohl's *Fantasmagorie.*

Windsor McCay produced perhaps his most famous film in 1914, *Gertie the Dinosaur.* But he also produced *The Sinking of the Lusitania* in 1918. The effects that McCay was able to imagine and achieve are, in my opinion, the best that had been done at the time—they would not be matched until the mid- to late-1930s. He truly was head and shoulders ahead of everyone else at the time (see Figure 1.3).

FIG 1.3 Windsor McCay's *The Sinking of the Lusitania.*

A typical animation desk setup was used in the early days of the animation process until the early 1920s. Windsor McCay set up his animation process like this, using tracing paper and transparent bond, so he could trace his backgrounds with each succeeding drawing (see Figure 1.4). Two holes punched in the paper would hold the paper in place, while the cross marks on the four corners were used to make certain all the drawings would line up as you animated each of the successive ones. You could use one method or the other, or both at once.

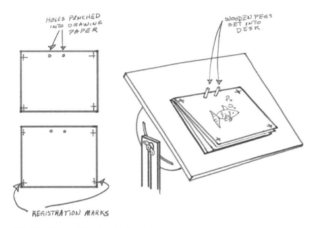

FIG 1.4 Windsor McCay's animation setup.

Meanwhile, within the industry there were advances in the way animation was being handled that advanced the medium. A French Canadian by the name of Raoul Barré and his partner Bill Nolan introduced the "peg" system. This would make it possible to register all drawings in exact alignment with each preceding and succeeding drawing, eliminating any shaking or giggling. The Barré–Nolan team also developed the long horizontal and vertical backgrounds. This would give the characters more freedom to move about the scenes without the need to trace the backgrounds onto each of the character drawings. It made it possible to use multiple layers of animated subjects and to incorporate effects in ways previously not possible, along with the introduction of the "cel system," attributed to John Randolph Bray and Earl Hurd, who patented the process in 1914. (The cel system consisted of clear celluloid sheets onto which drawings were traced on the front in ink and later painted on the back, filling in the interiors of the silhouetted characters.) Bray is also credited with the system for breaking down the work—the assembly line, if you will, of the layout department, background, animator, assistant, and so on. These innovations, along with the invention of the glass disk in the center of the animator's drawing board by Vernon George Stallings in the 1920s, further advanced the creative possibilities for animators. Now they could use a back light to see multiple levels at once and get precise one-to-one registration between characters as well as the effects around them (see Figure 1.5).

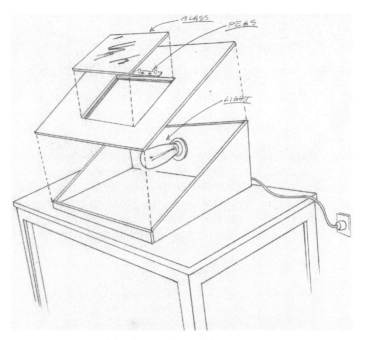

FIG 1.5 1920s animation desk with glass disk and box light.

After further innovations to the animation disk, it evolved into the more familiar-looking round disk that the animator could turn and adjust for a more comfortable drawing position. The animation disk had only top pegs until the mid- to late 1930s; the addition of bottom pegs came later and gave the animators the ability to plot pans (see Figures 1.6 and 1.7).

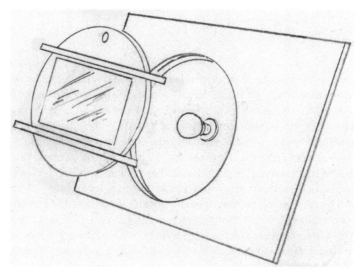

FIG 1.6 More familiar disk with top and bottom pegs.

FIG 1.7 My modern-day animation desk at Disney.

Animation started to rise to greater heights during the golden age of animation, roughly 1928–1967. Not only did the process get more sophisticated but also the stories got more complex in the telling and the visuals got more intricate. As the character animation became more sophisticated, the effects needed to rise to the occasion if they were to look and feel as if they belonged in the same environment as the characters, in order for the audience to believe that both effects and characters lived in the same environment. Otherwise the contrast would confuse the viewer and undermine the storytelling. In the mid- to late 1930s, a few effects specialists rose out of the character animation ranks. It was the Fleischer Studios and Walt Disney Studios that put more emphasis on the effects in their films. Disney led the way by using the series of shorts he made during that time. *Silly Symphonies* and the short *The Old Mill* used some ground-breaking innovations, such as the multiplane camera, that made for some truly memorable imagery. Disney not only used the shorts to train his character animators but also began training a small group of specialists with a knack for special effects. Early on, the Effects Department consisted of two animators and one assistant between them. Cyrus Young and Ugo D'orsi used their unique talents for animating effects to produce some of the best animated special effects ever done (see Figures 1.8 and 1.9).

FIG 1.8 "Sorcerer's Apprentice" from *Fantasia*, animated by Ugo D'orsi.

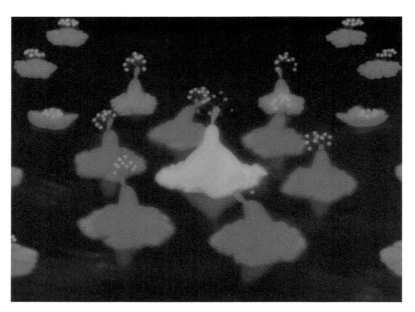

FIG 1.9 *Fantasia*, "Blossom Ballerina," animated by Cyrus Young.

These men, along with Josh Meador, who arrived in 1939 and who animated a lot of the water from the Monstro sequence in *Pinocchio*, raised the bar for effects done in Disney films. With the establishment of a department dedicated solely to doing effects in films, the character animators were given some breathing room and were free to fully concentrate their talents on character development and the acting aspects of their characters. The effects animators began studying film and high-speed photography of water, fire, mud, and anything related to the natural phenomenon that would be of use to them in producing realistic effects. This was done not for copying but for the study of patterns and design and the improvement of the overall quality of animated effects. Just as the character animators were studying anatomy and acting to improve their skills, the effects specialists studied all aspects of effects to prepare for the films that Walt Disney was planning.

Along with their realistic effects, they began experimenting with caricaturization of the effects to work not only with realistic effects for films like *Bambi* but cartoony films like *Dumbo*. The idea was that there needed to be a marriage of characters and effects so that each style could be represented in the same world environment. Whether the effect was realistic or cartoony, however, it needed to follow real-world physics. This was true even when it was comically employed in a scene as a caricatured representation of itself or as stylized as a Mary Blair design or even the more contemporary films from the second golden age of animation, roughly 1989–1999 (see Figures 1.10 through 1.12).

For a long time it was always pencil on paper and those drawings would then be transferred, using pen and ink, onto celluloid sheets and painted on the backside of those cels in black and white. Three-strip Technicolor was introduced in 1932 in Disney's *Flowers and Trees*. Later, in the late 1950s, Ub Iwerks at Disney applied the use of the xerography process, by which the drawing are copied onto the cels and then painted on the back of the cels. Today's digital tools have given us another option where the drawings done on paper are scanned into a digital file and painted on computers using an ink and paint program to color and manipulate those elements. Another new option given to the artist today is the use of a stylus by which the artist can now draw directly on a digital tablet and replace the pencil and paper steps.

FIG 1.10 Disney's *Johnny Appleseed.*

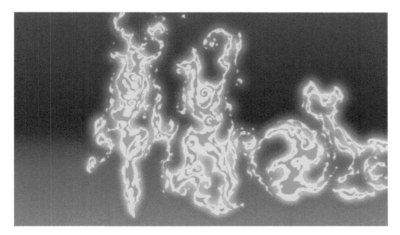

FIG 1.11 Disney's *Aladdin.*

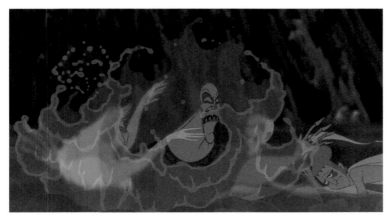

FIG 1.12 Disney's *Hercules.*

Being able to do the drawings as well as the backgrounds digitally has given filmmakers another tool to produce films. Focus and diffusion or intensity of color or the blending and combining multiple levels of characters and effects within a shot is now pretty much a one-stop process (see Figure 1.13).

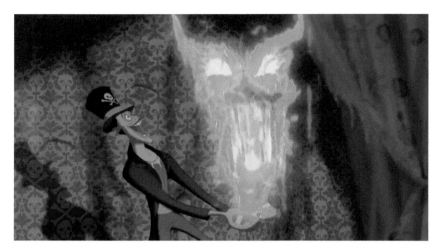

FIG 1.13 Disney's *The Princess and the Frog*.

The same process that used to be done in an optical printer with numerous strips of film for each element is now fully completed on a computer, giving filmmakers a faster process by which to composite shots with multiple elements and a myriad of special effects tools. The process is essentially the same. The tools may be different, but it still all has to start with the artist and the drawing!

CHAPTER 2

What Exactly Is a Traditionally Animated Effect?

It's not what you look at that matters, it's what you see!

—*Henry David Thoreau*

Traditionally, effects animation in a film would be anything that is not a character—everything from a stick being kicked by a character to the water that the stick falls into and the splash that it causes. A flood, a tornado, smoke, fire, snow, or magical effects. The shadows from a character on the ground as well as the tones that emphasize that character's volume and form! An effects animator is a specialist within the specialized field of animation—someone who possesses a good understanding of how things work in the physical world and of natural phenomena. He or she should also have a pretty good understanding of physics and analytic skills, which will help in breaking down the how and the why of an effect and then interpreting that effect into a drawing that gives the illusion of being a real splash of water or smoke rising from a campfire and so on.

As in character animation, an effects animator should be able to draw well, with a penchant for design and a love for environmental events—you know, the guy you see staring into the churning waters at the base of an ocean-side cliff or the crackling fire in a fire pit! The guy who watches how the water drips off his arm while standing in a swimming pool or how the waves leave patterns while receding and leaving cauliflower-like designs of foam on the shore. Or the girl who watches TV for documentaries on lava and volcanoes erupting and observes the patterns that are made from fire escapes casting shadows onto the wall of a building. In other words an observer of things happening every day, all around us, that others may take for granted or take no notice of whatsoever! Someone with a visual acuity for details and a knack for translating that visually, in a series of drawings that emulates the look and feel of that effect. I think we all have this information packed away in our brains.

We have all seen these things in our lifetimes and some have paid more attention to them than others. You just have to train yourself to recall what you've witnessed and build on that information utilizing those memories as well as your imagination in your animation. Reflections on a wall cast from the sun bouncing off a puddle of water and the rhythms they impart on your senses is a memory you can call upon when you need to add a little ambiance to a shot where a couple of lovers are looking soulfully into each other's eyes, to add to the tender moment and enhance the romantic atmosphere. This is all part of an animator's visual recall, ready to be used whenever the need may arise. All that is required is for you to remember what you've seen and when and where to apply it.

It would behoove you to study and familiarize yourself with these natural phenomena, which may give you more insight into the forces you will be dealing with as you animate effects and will assure that the effects will follow the natural principals of the real world. No matter what the design or art direction of the film is, effects need to act and feel as if they are acting under real-world principles!

- *Physics*: The natural science that involves the study of matter and its motion through space and time.
- *Energy*: A property of objects, transferable among them via fundamental interactions, which can be converted into different forms but not created or destroyed.
- *Force*: An interaction that tends to change the motion of an object. A force can cause a mass to change its velocity.
- *Inertia*: The resistance of any physical object to any change in its state of motion, including change in its speed and direction. The tendency of an object to move in a straight line at a constant velocity.
- *Gravity*: Gives weight to physical objects and causes them to fall toward one another. A natural phenomenon by which physical bodies attract each other.
- *Trajectory*: The path followed by a projectile under the action of a given force.
- *Momentum*: The mass and velocity of an object. The momentum of an object remains constant unless acted upon by an outside force.
- *Friction*: Surface resistance to relative motion.
- *Perspective*: The art of drawing solid objects on a two-dimensional surface so as to give the right impression of the height, width, depth, and position in relation to each other when viewed from a particular point.

Knowledge of the forces that are prominent in nature is required as an effects animator. Why? Understanding why gravity, for instance, plays a part in the trajectory of an object traveling through the air, as do friction and inertia, helps you to animate it in a realistic fashion! A ball thrown across a field is carried through the air because of the momentum at which it was thrown. Inertia keeps it going until gravity pulls on it and friction in the air slows it down, causing the ball to follow an arc in its path in the air across the field (see Figure 2.1).

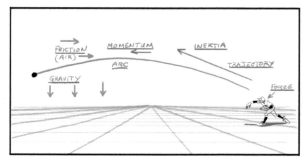

FIG 2.1 Forces affecting trajectory (arcs).

CHAPTER 3

What Does It Take to Become an Effects Animator?

The more we study the more we discover our ignorance!

—*Percy Bysshe Shelley*

Let me start off by first saying that no matter how long and how hard you work at your craft, you will never know everything! This is not meant to discourage you but to make you understand that no matter what it is that you want to master, you never will. There will always be new ideas, newer technology, newer or better techniques! They will come from people like you and how much you push your particular envelope. So make sure you never stop pushing yourself and that you challenge yourself in all your endeavors. Settling on one way of doing things will only serve to stymie the creative process. Besides, it's not as much fun that way!

It's not just important to look at something but also to study why it behaves the way it does and how it interacts with the surroundings. For example, the consistency of a liquid, be it oil, water, or honey, is important to note. The viscosity of the liquid will make it flow differently over a surface like a wooden table. Water will flow and spread faster over the wooden surface of that table than will the spilling of honey or oil. These details are important to get right when animating them. If a character in a scene spills a glass of water on the table and the water moves like honey, the audience may be distracted from what is happening in the scene, wondering why that water is moving so slowly. Will the liquid morph into some otherworldly creature that grows and attacks the character? Or bubble and eat through the table for some reason? In other words, it may take the viewer's attention away from what the character is doing and disrupt the flow of continuity in the story! Unless the story line specifically directs for the liquid to hold the audience's attention for a specific story point, the water just becomes a peripheral occurrence where a character has clumsily spilled water on the table out of nervousness or clumsiness while going about his acting tasks. No more, no less!

Water should flow like water and not honey, and mud should flow and have the consistency and weight that is associated with a thick dirt and water mix and not plain water. What does that mean in terms of animating those elements? It's all in the timing of the thing as well as the design of it. This is learned through observation and practice, practice, practice—applying what you have observed and studied!

You should strive for simplicity in design and to animate volume and mass, not just lines that delineate the element from a two-dimensional point of view. You need to concern yourself with how a splash looks and feels in three dimensions as a volume and a mass of water, not just a flat drawing that doesn't indicate that the splash is not only radiating up and down but coming toward you as well as away from you. Hence this is why it is important to understand *perspective*. Draw in all axes, *x*, *y*, and *z*, relative to the background setting. Figure 3.1a is flat and two-dimensional, concerned only with the *x* and *y* axes. Figure 3.1b is a fuller dimensional drawing, staying true to the perspective and clearly delineating all *x*, *y*, and *z* axes.

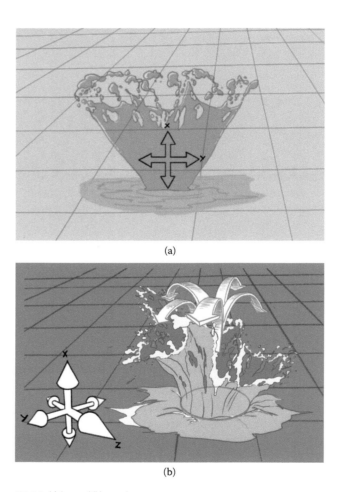

(a)

(b)

FIG 3.1 (a) Axes and (b) axes planes.

Even though water is transparent, it has mass and volume. A splash that occurs when a pebble is dropped into a pool of water will not only look different from a boulder falling into a pool of water but will move with different timing due to the volume and mass of the amount of water being displaced.

The more attention given to these details will mean the difference between a successful effect and a failed one! (see Figure 3.2).

(a)   (b)

FIG 3.2 (a) Small-scale and (b) large-scale splashes.

So, what am I asking you to do in order to be a successful effects animator? Draw and study what you observe! The more you draw, the easier it will be for you to animate the effect you're striving for.

Knowing what it is that you are going to animate and what you want the desired effect to do should be the hard part; the drawing of it is the easy part if your draftsmanship is good. So, perfect your drawing!

Draw each and every day! How do you do that? Easy! Carry a sketchbook with you at all times. You never know what you will come in contact with or what events you will be witness to. Draw anything and everything! Landscapes or details of textures, such as the bark of a tree or stone walls. The more you know the easier it will be to recall and duplicate. Pay attention to the details and how they work and fit in context to the surroundings. Sketching also forces you to study the element that you're drawing. Keep it loose and gestural, keeping in mind the movement and timing that you're witnessing. Jot down notes next to your sketches. More than a few animated effects have failed due to poor draftsmanship. Don't let that be you—draw! Remember, if you understand the problem you will also have the solution. The more you practice, the more you draw, the more you fill those memory banks in your brain, the easier it will be for you to solve problems in the future. Greater knowledge of your discipline will make your problem-solving a cinch. Stumbling blocks will most definitely crop up as you animate! It's always best to be prepared for the unexpected issues by expecting them.

Effects are part of the environment, in a scene, helping to establish the ambiance within that setting. The knowledge accumulated over a lifetime of observation of all things around you will make you able to produce whatever is required in a scene. But observation is key! Notice that I keep bringing that up. It must be important! No worries, it's all out there for you to study, for free. All you have to do is observe.

When you go out and draw, draw from life as much as possible! There is nothing wrong with drawing while watching TV or from the Internet, but there are factors that you experience when drawing from life that cannot be duplicated in a video file. The rumbling under your feet as the waves come crashing onto shore and the spray washes across your face. These are sensations that you can't get through your TV or computer screen. The heat radiating from a fire and the smell of wood burning and crackling. All these and more are sensations that your senses are privy to that you can't get from a book filled with photographs of fire. These sensations will play a part as you animate them on paper, recalling those sensations will add a dimension to those drawings that would be missed if you had not lived that experience of sketching from life. That said, I will not diminish the great part that video and film references play in animation! Study all you can and store it all in your head so that you can bring up those files in your mind's eye whenever the need arises.

Caricaturing the effect is an important practice while animating your effects. "Keep it simple" is something to keep in mind: Never fall in love with a pretty drawing of water, fire, or smoke! The important thing is to animate the effect, not to spend 3 months on a splash getting every single detail of that splash. The audience doesn't need to see every single highlight or droplet of a splash, so be objective in the details. If that "pretty" drawing hinders the overall flow of your animation, it becomes superfluous and you need to pull it! Go ahead and mount and frame it if you want, but it has no place in your animation if it is out of place with the rest of your animation. Think in terms of what is important in the scene. You have to learn to be your own editor. Determine what will work and what won't.

How much detail is enough or too much? This will play a big role as you come to understand about deadlines and time management. Give your element a history—what was it doing before your scene and what will happen to it next? Make sure you know the story line, the scene before yours, and the one that follows so that all the scenes work smoothly and consistently throughout. All the effects should look like they are from the same universe and relate to all the other effects in the film.

A musician practices scales and timing every day, until it's part of his system and he doesn't even have to think about it because it becomes second nature, especially if he wants to get better at his art. There is no substitute for this! Learn everything you can and practice. Keeping all that in mind, an effects animator should know certain basic things that eventually become second nature as you animate. Here are some things to keep in mind that you will want to study and perfect as you move forward in your pursuit of becoming an effects animator.

- *Design*: When designing, start out with simple gesture drawings! You should never be happy with your first drawing/design, even if that's the one you eventually settle on. Remember, the basic principles of animation apply—squash and stretch, overlapping action, drag, and follow-through for the animation phase to come later on. Take into account the forces that will be affecting the element you're going to animate—the surface lines indicating the surface or texture, the density, shading, or color separations. The more thought you put into your initial designs, the stronger and more successful your design will be. The hard part comes when you break it down to the basic shapes and simplification of the element in order to bring it to a more favorable design that can be more convenient to animate and still keep the integrity of your design! And always remember that you need to coordinate with the art director on the film to be sure of maintaining a cohesion of design throughout the look of the film. Of course, final approval will come with the director (see Figure 3.3).
- *Timing*: Whether you intend your timing to be realistic or to caricature it for comedic reasons, or even when "cartooning" an effect, such as giving the effect a character-like personality, may give you some freedom, always keep the "natural principles" or real-world physics laws in the back of your mind. Timing and the perfection of it will come with time and experience! This will take patience and practice. So don't pass over this discipline too lightly. Timing in animation is critical! Understand that not everything you're animating happens all at the same time. Especially when animating natural or environmental effects—fire, water, smoke, lava—this is where overlapping action, drag, and follow-through are critical. While some parts of an element are going up vertically, others may be starting to travel down or horizontally. Even timing is not very pleasing to look at. Nothing in nature moves uniformly! It seems that a certain level of asymmetry in the design and timing of an effect always makes it more pleasing to look at, at least in my humble opinion. Remember, even timing is boring! I'll be going over further timing points later on.

FIG 3.3 The director always has the last word.

- *Perspective*: Construction of your effects to fit your layout or background is important in whatever you're doing. Whether you are animating a box, a rock, or a splash, if your perspective is flawed that element will fail. Everything works in relation to everything else around it.

If your perspective is faulty and your ellipses are wrong while doing a splash effect, it won't "fit" right in your background. The greater your understanding and mastering of perspective, the more successful your drawings and the quality of your work will be.

- *Volumes*: Maintain the same proportions of an object or an effect throughout the duration of a shot.
- *Silhouette*: Clearly define believable shapes in the element you're animating. The clear use of positive and negative shapes while staging your drawings against your layout will further serve to clearly define what it is you are portraying. Use of straight and curved lines will also help to define the dynamics of your drawings. Make sure to never lose sight of the construction of your drawing. The shapes and line work should be consistent throughout. If you start out using thick and thin lines, make sure your line work is consistent. Don't fluctuate from thick and thin to a flat and even line (see Figure 3.4).

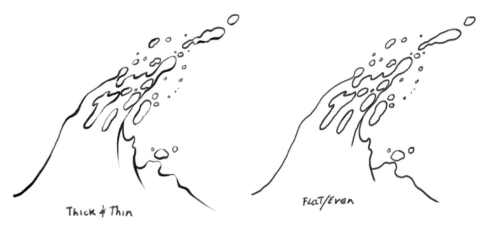

FIG 3.4 Thick and thin versus flat/even line work.

Common Terminology

I will be covering these more in depth later on but here is some terminology to keep in mind.

- *Extremes, Breakdowns, and Inbetweens*: Step-by-step progression in the animation process.
- *Arcs*: The curve of a path of action along which an object travels.
- *Thumbnails*: Small, rough drawings that help you stage and plan your animation.
- *Straight Ahead and Pose to Pose*: Methods of animating an action.
- *Primary Action*: The dominant or initial action of an animation.
- *Secondary Action*: The minor actions that follow those of a primary action.
- *Exposure Sheet*: The worksheet containing production number, sequence, scene number, director notes, dialogue, camera, layout, frame count, and animation drawings exposure. In other words, an accounting of everything concerning a scene that accompanies all layout and animation drawings throughout the production pipeline.
- *Overlap*: The action that occurs when the primary action of a mass or volume overruns the primary action once it has reached the apex of its action or changes direction.

- *Follow-Through*: The continuation of an action that results once the primary action has changed direction.
- *Drag*: The very tip, or most extreme ends, of those shapes that arc behind the path of action described by the primary and secondary action.
- *Flipping*: The technique of flipping between two animation drawings with the third or "inbetween" drawing in the topmost position in order to check whether the movement is correct. The first drawing (1) is placed on the bottom, the third (3) on top of the first, and the inbetween drawing (2) on the top; flip them in the order 1–2–3–2–1–2–3–2–1 and keep that rhythm until you're satisfied that the action is correct.
- *Rolling Drawings*: The technique of using your non–drawing hand to check the animation of four to five drawings at a time. Rolling the animation paper in a smooth rolling action from the first drawing on the bottom through each successive drawing stacked on top of each other (1, 2, 3, 4, 5), the animator is able to determine whether the movement in the animation is following through properly to the action that is desired and whether the arcs are smooth and true to the animation.
- *Tones*: The shadowed areas on a character that defines its volume and shape using a key light source from the background lighting to determine the placement.
- *Tone for Rim*: The use of a tone to extract a rim light or highlight on a character.
- *Cast Tone*: A shadow cast onto a character from another character or an object.
- *Highlight or Rim Light*: Again, using a prominent key light source from the background painting (usually a strong back light) to determine a highlight or rim light on a character.
- *Drop Shadow*: The shadow cast from a character onto the ground plane directly below him.
- *Cast Shadow*: The shadow cast from a character onto the ground at an angle.
- *Truck*: A camera move involving "pushing in or out or laterally" in a shot, maintaining focus on a character or an effect.
- *North–South Move*: A camera move in a shot that involves travel up or down in the x-axis.
- *East–West Move*: A camera move in a shot that involves travel left or right in the y-axis.
- *Top and Bottom Pegs*: Peg bars located at the top and bottom of an animation disk. They can work independently of each other to move horizontally left or right. These are used when an animated character or effect move across the screen. By synchronizing the move of the top pegs (the background) and the bottom pegs (the character/effect), this technique prevents the "sliding" that occurs when the background moves at a greater increment from frame to frame than does the animated element. The animated element is normally drawn on the bottom pegs.
- *Dissolve*: Fading in or out of a scene, usually by fading one shot out while simultaneously fading in the next scene.
- *Wipe*: Transitioning from one scene to another by using a negative matte and moving it across the screen left or right, diagonally, or north or south.
- *Negative or Positive Matte*: An image or shape on a frame that is either a clear opening or solid shape that can be used to block out or expose another image in a shot.

CHAPTER 4

Thumbnails

Plan your work and work your plan!

—Unknown

Before you start to animate, think about your shot! First, are there continuity issues? Do you need to match with the shot that comes before or after yours? Check out those scenes on the storyboards or the story reel. Talk to the director or the lead person that passed the scene to you to animate. What instructions did you get? Take notes if you have to. Do you need to see the animator that did the other scenes? Once you've answered all those questions and are clear as to any particular design specifications, then you can start! (see Figure 4.1).

(a)   (b)

FIG 4.1 (a) Continuity. (b) Storyboards.   *(Continued)*

(c)

FIG 4.1 (Continued) (c) Story reel.

Where do you start? First, you think! What is involved? Are there characters involved where you have to be aware of registration? What about scale? Thumbnail the action out, paying attention to your composition. Do as many thumbnails as you need to cover the shot from start to finish. These are quick little gesture drawings to plan the staging of your shot and your animation; there is no need to make finished, detailed drawings (see Figure 4.2).

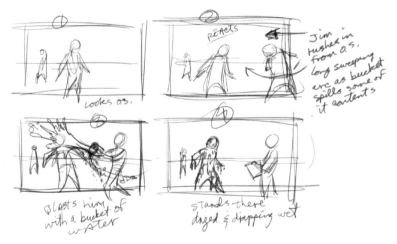

FIG 4.2 Thumbnails.

Don't settle for your first plan! Are there other ways you can do the shot? Try them out in your thumbnails. The more time spent on your planning, the more easily the animation will go. Scribble down some notes on the sketches of what you want to be doing in the shot. It doesn't hurt to jot down ideas, especially if you're like me and have a great idea that you forget 10 minutes later! (see Figure 4.3).

While staging your shot, decide on your primary and secondary actions. Can the animation be done in different layers so you can separate the levels for ease of animation by doing them one at a time? This can be a huge time saver in the long run! (see Figure 4.4).

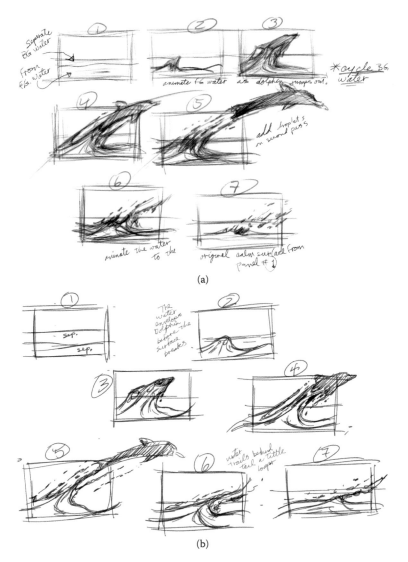

FIG 4.3 (a) Thumbnail version 1 (simple). (b) Thumbnail version 2 (more design).

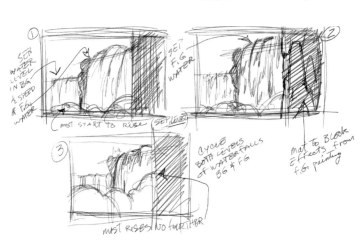

FIG 4.4 Waterfall Breakdown.

What is the perspective in your shot and how will it affect the animation of foreground and background effects elements? What should you animate first? Thumbnails are a great planning tool that should be utilized in planning your effects animation (see Figure 4.5).

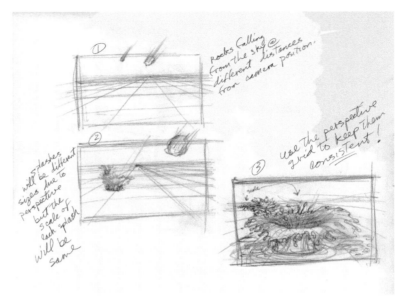

FIG 4.5 Thumbnails (perspective considerations).

You should also look at your thumbnails as a road map, one that shows you many ways to arrive at your final destination. The directions may change as you do your animation, and you should be open to navigating in a new direction if the animation drives you there. Thumbnails should be an approximation of where to start and where you want to go with you effects. But again, the animation may take a turn or a twist as you're animating. Things may present themselves that, although purely accidental, can work to your advantage and you may want to go in that direction. At least be open to it and don't be afraid to try something new (see Figure 4.6).

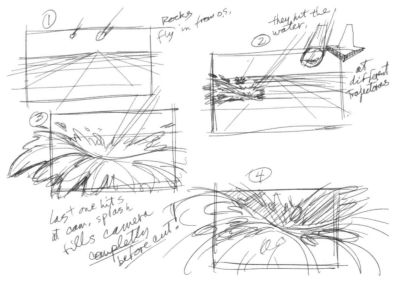

FIG 4.6 Thumbnails (try something different).

CHAPTER 5

Caricaturing of an Effect

Simplicity is the glory of expression.

—Walt Whitman

To caricature something or someone is simply to exaggerate its characteristics or to distort and imitate it. How can we caricature an effect? We must first start with what it really looks like, then bend and distort its most prominent features. A cartoonist would exaggerate the features of a man or woman's face by drawing a large nose, large eyes, or a receding hairline that recedes much further than it actually does or by exaggerating a tall and skinny frame to stick-like legs and a tiny torso to emphasize those areas, and so on. The caricature could end up wearing pants that are too short and baggy for him and having drooping shoulders because he always has to bend down to speak with people much shorter than he. But the cartoonist does something else: he takes those features that stand out on that person and simplifies them and eliminates all the other details. Such is the case of caricaturing an effect. A splash of water could have overly large shapes and drops.

Let's start with what would be considered a realistic drawing of a water splash (Figure 5.1). Here the water has struck a rock and not only is splashing up and over the rock but also is flowing around the obstacle. Thus, I have used some shapes on the eddy side to indicate ripples that will move in the direction of the current—that is, left to right. Even though we're caricaturing the water, we must always make sure that it maintains the qualities that make it look and move like water.

FIG 5.1 Water splash.

Now let's redraw over the original drawing and simplify it. Use the existing silhouette and remove some of those detail to minimize the intricacies of the realistic-looking water. You simplify without losing the feel of your animation, retaining the impression that this is still water (see Figure 5.2).

FIG 5.2 Water splash simplified.

Once you've done that, go over it again. Remember, never be satisfied with only one or two examples! Keep removing the detail that makes it a realistic-looking drawing of water—use only the bare essentials and keep the dynamics that keep it flowing over the rock and splashing upward. Combine many of the small details, such as the drops, into larger globs and remove the rest (see Figure 5.3).

FIG 5.3 Water splash simplified more.

Let's try the same thing with fire. We can give it a personality—fire can suddenly develop legs and start chasing another character around the room, lashing out with a lick of flames that resemble arms. So let's start once again with what might appear a realistic-looking fire (Figure 5.4).

FIG 5.4 Fire.

Now let's simplify that and go even further. Figure 5.5 gives the fire a much simpler color scheme, with blocks of color and no blending or rendering on the flames.

(a)   (b)

FIG 5.5 (a) Fire simplified. (b) Fire simplified with color separations.

When you have to animate an effect that may have to look like it has arms and legs, don't overthink it! Start with a simple stick figure (Figure 5.6a); no details are needed at this point. If the "fire demon" is chasing someone, draw a simple character running, then go over that stick figure and encase him in fire (Figure 5.6b). Make sure that fire casing maintains a consistent volume. While you can have licks of flames coming off the creature, you don't want him to change his volume from one drawing to another. Finally, remove the stick figures to reveal your final image (Figure 5.6c).

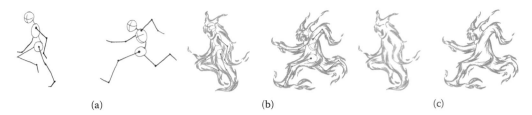

FIG 5.6 (a) Stick figures running. (b) Fire with legs and arms; (c) Final Image.

Can we not do the same with smoke? Let's give the smoke arms with which to engulf a character in a scene (see Figure 5.7).

FIG 5.7 Smoke.

Now take that smoke from Figure 5.8 and alter him to give him arm-like appendages, but keep him anchored to the fire source on the ground.

FIG 5.8 Smoke with arms.

It's just a matter of using your imagination and portraying the effect with a particular personality that gives emphasis to the nature of the elements involved or simplifying to the simplest basic shapes without losing the identity of what it is and what it does.

Of course, all of this is led by the story and by how the art director and director want to tell it. If it's a cartoon that treats the effects as personalities, you as an effects animator may be given a lot of freedom with the design and how the effects are animated.

In films like *Aladdin* and *Hercules*, the effects were complex, pulling design elements from the calligraphy of the region or the amphora of the time. A more recent film, *Song of the Sea*, had a much simpler and more childlike look in the design of the backgrounds, characters, and of course the effects. Everything came together to make a cohesive, visually stunning film with the charm of a beautifully illustrated children's book (see Figure 5.9).

FIG 5.9 *Song of the Sea.*

CHAPTER 6

Perspective

What is once well done, is done forever.

—*Henry David Thoreau*

Perspective is the art of drawing solid objects on a two-dimensional surface so as to give the impression of their height, width, depth, and position in relation to each other when viewed from a particular point. In other words, it's a way of showing depth or distance in a drawing or painting by making objects that are further from the viewer smaller and those that are closer, larger (Google and Merriam-Webster). Why is it important to know? Read the above once again!

This goes back to the need to draw well in order to be a good animator, whether an effects or character animator. But why do you need to know it and know it well as an effects animator? Let's take a scene that may come to you from the layout department that requires you to animate a truck on a road traveling toward camera. The scene comes to the effects department before going to the character animator, because the truck needs to be animated first so that the character can be animated inside the vehicle. Usually the layout would have a rough indication of the vehicle's first and final position. It would then be your job to animate the truck from the first pose to the last, with all the characteristics of a truck going over a road. If the layout has no perspective grid for you to work with, it's up to you to draw one for your reference. This is important so that the truck moves in proper scale from its first to last position. You need to be able to keep the truck size consistent throughout the animation. The best way to do this is by making a guide that sets up the path that the truck will travel and then animating to that path.

We start with the layout drawing of the landscape with the road and the rough truck drawings (see Figure 6.1).

FIG 6.1 Layout with key truck positions.

The first step is to set up the horizon line. On a separate piece of paper laid on top of the layout drawing, find the horizon and draw a line on your paper all the way across. Use a T-square, triangle, and straight edge to be as accurate as possible if you can. Also using the bottom of the tires of the truck as a guide, draw a line (a) to the horizon line to find the vanishing point number (1). Now draw a line (b) from where the front tires touch the ground to the horizon line to get the vanishing point number (2). You may need to use an extension on your paper to find this! (see Figure 6.2).

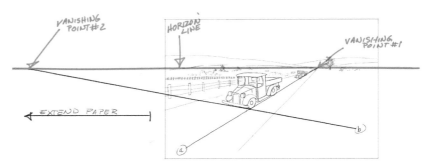

FIG 6.2 Horizon line and vanishing points.

Do the same now using the top of the truck roof (c and d). Then, drawing two perpendicular lines from the intersecting points of those lines, you can now find the front plane of the truck (e and f) (see Figure 6.3).

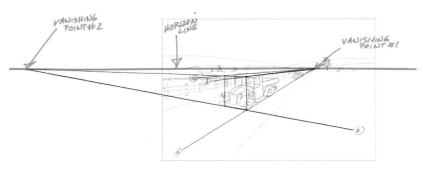

FIG 6.3 Define the front plane of the truck.

On the front plane drawing, draw two diagonal lines from the top and bottom corners to find the center of the rectangle and further define the plane (see Figure 6.4).

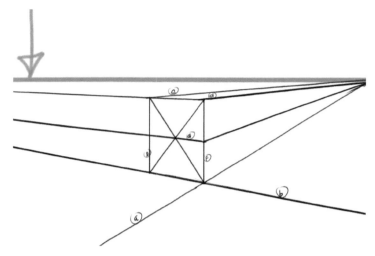

FIG 6.4 Detail path and size guide.

The center point can now be used to draw another line (g) to the vanishing points (1) and (2) (see Figure 6.5).

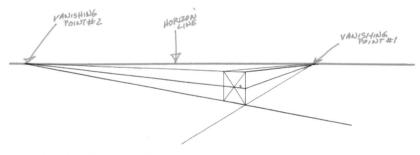

FIG 6.5 Front plane with diagonals and center line.

Now draw a perpendicular line through that same center point of the plane (h) (see Figure 6.6).

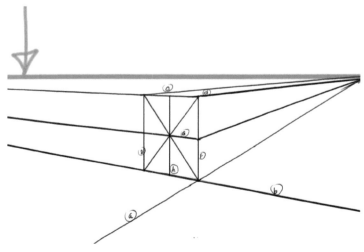

FIG 6.6 Detail path and size guide (next step).

You now need to draw a vertical line that intersects the horizontal line at a 90-degree angle at vanishing point (1) to help establish vanishing point (3). Using the rear corners of the truck, draw two perpendicular lines (i and j) that intersect the lines drawn from the top and bottom of the truck to the vanishing point (1). Now draw a diagonal line (k) through the corners of the newly formed rectangle all the way to the new vertical line. Where these intersect will be your new vanishing point (3). From here on, draw a perpendicular line from the point of intersection of each line (d) and the diagonals (l) you draw in the succeeding diagonals and perpendicular lines (m) drawn to vanishing point (3) (see Figure 6.7).

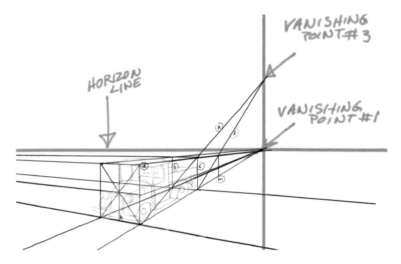

FIG 6.7 Establish vanishing point (3) for scale.

Continue doing this as far back as Position 1 of your truck layout or for as many as may be needed for the shot (see Figure 6.8).

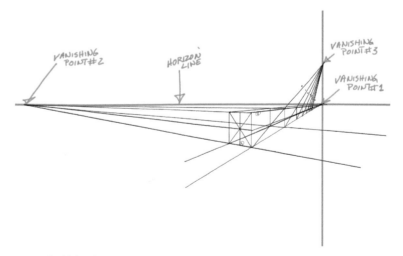

FIG 6.8 Establish scale in perspective.

Next, draw a line from where line (j) intersects line (a) to the vanishing point (2). The distance described in z is the length of the truck. Do the same with each perpendicular line you draw using the diagonals to line (a). See lines (n, o, p, q, and r). The final thing you need to do is draw a line (y) from the center vertical line (h) on the front plane to the vanishing point (1). This will be your ground plane to which you animate the truck, assuring you that the truck will travel in a straight line down through its projected path (see Figure 6.9).

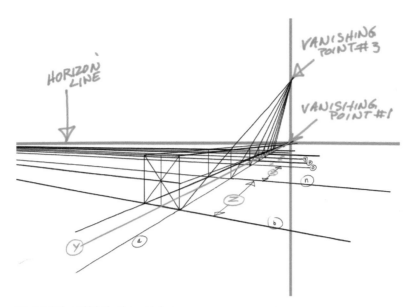

FIG 6.9 Scale established with ground plane.

Each cube represents the size of the truck, height, width, and length. Now you will be able to animate that truck knowing that it will work properly and in the correct perspective for your shot (see Figure 6.10).

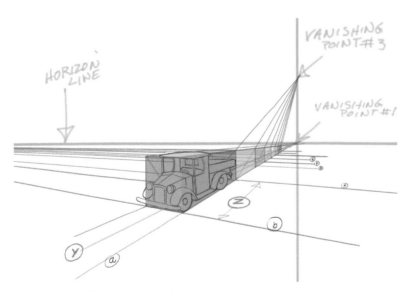

FIG 6.10 Scale complete with animation path.

Many people have their own ways of drawing out perspective grids and I have mine. It's no better or worse than any other way, and there are many books on the market that you can pick up and learn more precise methods. I'll show you how I do it, and what has worked for me. Try as many methods as you can until you find the easiest and best way that works for you. But don't skimp on learning perspective! This is a "must know." You will see how important it is as you read on in this book for many effects issues. Here, I'll give you a more common example showing how easy it is to make perspective mistakes, especially with the misuse of ellipses, and how I've learned to resolve the problem.

Let's say one day you get a scene deposited on your desk of a lake where fish are jumping out of the water at varying distances from shore. You will need to animate those splashes so the fish that are jumping out of the water in the distance will have splashes that will relate properly to their scale (no pun intended), as will the splashes of the fish that are closer to camera (see Figure 6.11).

FIG 6.11 Lake layout.

The fish are all approximately the same size but are at varying distances from shore, and the splashes they make in their acrobatic efforts would be essentially the same scale. You want to draw a perspective grid over the water surface from shore to the horizon so that you'll be able to draw your ellipses correctly, as you set about animating the splashes so that they and the fish are at the same scale.

Again, you start by drawing the horizon line (a) (usually at eye level), a perpendicular line (b) that's at 90 degrees to the horizon line, and a horizontal line (c) at the bottom of the picture parallel to the horizon line. Be as accurate as possible using a T-square and triangle (see Figure 6.12).

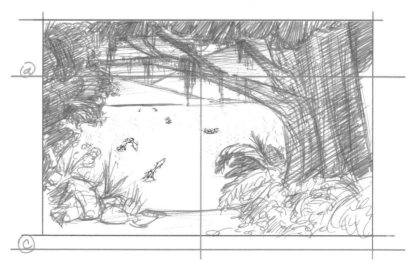

FIG 6.12 Horizontal and vertical guides.

On the bottom line (c), make marks of equal spacing from the center line (b); in this case I have them marked as numbers 1 through 7 (see Figure 6.13).

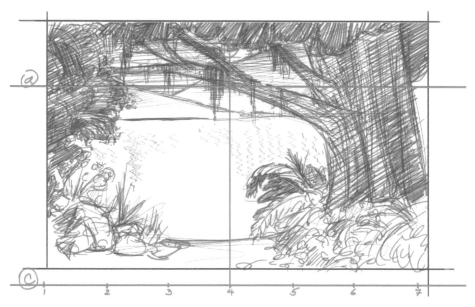

FIG 6.13 Equal spacers.

Now, using those marks draw vertical lines, top to bottom (see Figure 6.14).

FIG 6.14 Draw vertical lines.

Using the point where lines (a) and (b) cross as your vanishing point, draw perspective lines to the points marked 1 through 7 on line (c) (see Figure 6.15).

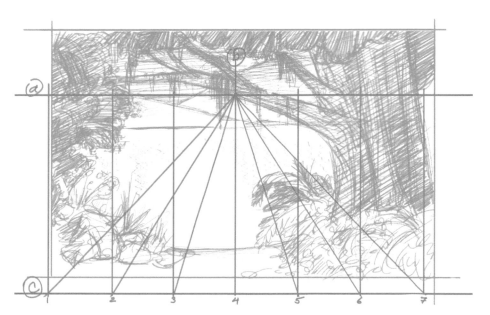

FIG 6.15 Diagonal lines to the vanishing point.

Now draw a diagonal line (d) from Point 7 on line (c) to where line (a) and vertical line 1 meet (see Figure 6.16).

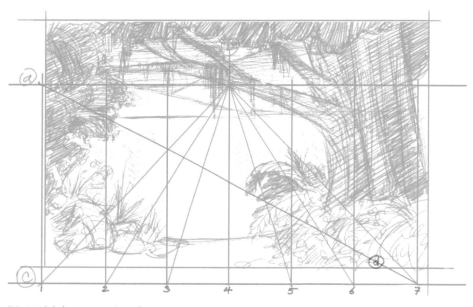

FIG 6.16 Lake layout perspective grid.

As accurately as you can, draw a horizontal line (e) from where the diagonal line (d) crosses the perspective line 6 parallel to lines (c) and (a) (see Figure 6.17).

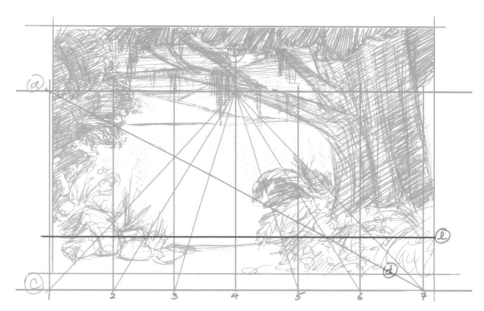

FIG 6.17 Draw horizontal lines.

Continue drawing horizontal lines, using the points where the diagonal line (d) crosses the perspective lines of 5, 4, 3, 2, and 1 (see Figure 6.18).

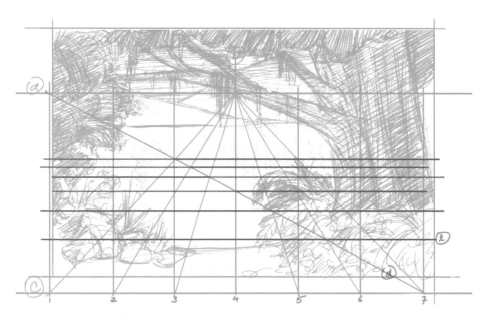

FIG 6.18 Continue horizontal lines.

Looks like we're running out of room, but have no fear! Using the vanishing point, where lines (a) and (b) intersect, continue drawing the perspective line to where vertical line 1 is intersected by the horizontal lines you have just drawn, so that you can finish your grid (see Figure 6.19).

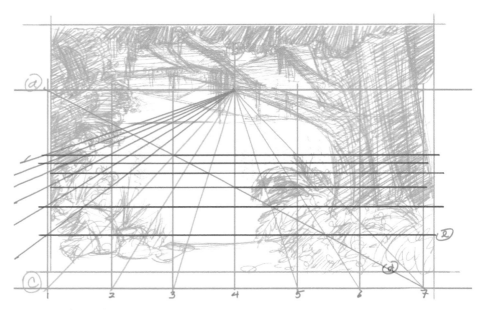

FIG 6.19 Draw horizontal to the top.

Finish drawing horizontal lines using the points where line (d) intersects with your newly drawn perspective lines, to the far side of the lake shore of your layout drawing (see Figure 6.20).

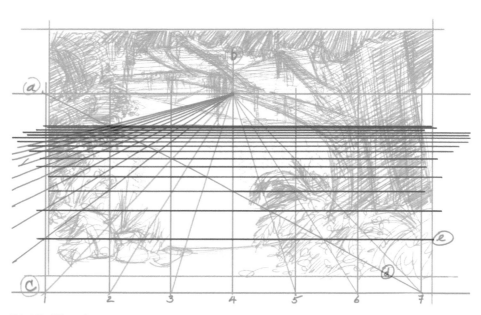

FIG 6.20 Grid complete.

Now that our grid is complete, we can start on the fun stuff. Laying a new piece of animation paper on top of our grid drawing and the animated fish one by one in sequential order we can start animating our water splash effects. We start with laying down rough ellipses at the point of the fish jumping out of the water or splashing back into it (see Figure 6.21).

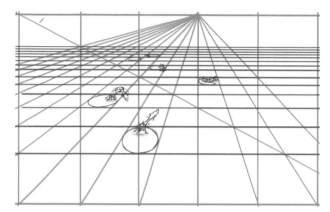

FIG 6.21 Fit ellipses in grid.

After drawing your rough perspective grid, draw the rough ellipses (see Figure 6.22).

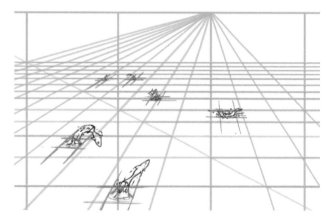

FIG 6.22 Rough ellipses.

Should the positions of the fish and the grid not line up to make it easy to draw the ellipses within the grids, have no fear. With the grid in place, roughly draw lines parallel to the lines on the grid as close to the areas affected with fish jumping out of or into the water as possible.

Now sit back and look at your overall perspective grid and determine whether the ellipses work together (see Figure 6.23).

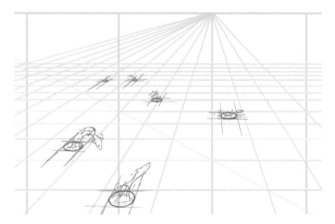

FIG 6.23 Overall perspective grid.

If the ellipses work, then you can begin designing the water splashes and start animating (see Figure 6.24).

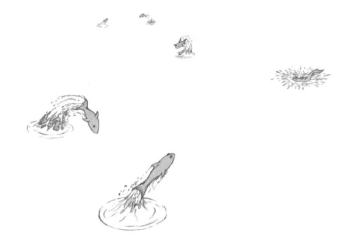

FIG 6.24 Layout effects design.

Your final animation now works with your background (see Figure 6.25).

FIG 6.25 Layout without grid.

Before ending this chapter, I want to go over something that will help you in drawing ellipses from a perspective grid, once you have your perspective established (see Figure 6.26).

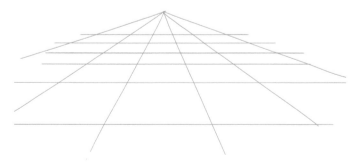

FIG 6.26 Ellipses.

You can draw your ellipses within your grid by first dissecting the shapes you've drawn out in your grid. First, draw diagonal lines (a to c, b to d) from the four corners to get the center in your figure (see Figure 6.27).

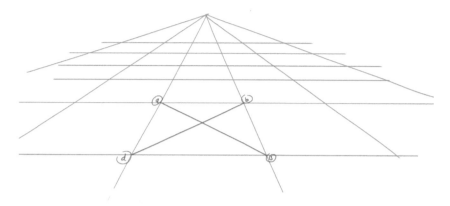

FIG 6.27 Ellipses.

Now dissect the shape with vertical and horizontal lines (e and f) (see Figure 6.28).

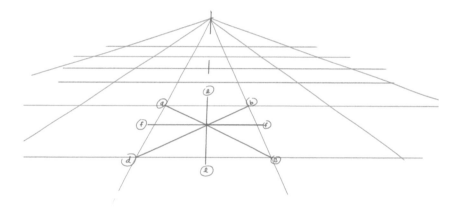

FIG 6.28 Ellipses.

Now draw lines to connect points e to f, creating a diamond shape (see Figure 6.29).

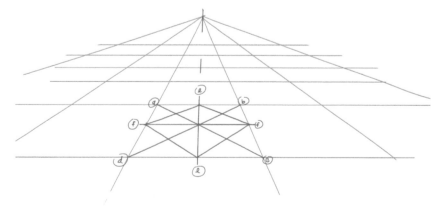

FIG 6.29 Ellipses.

On the diagonal lines (a to c) and (b to d), mark off the center between lines (e to f) and the corners (see Figure 6.30).

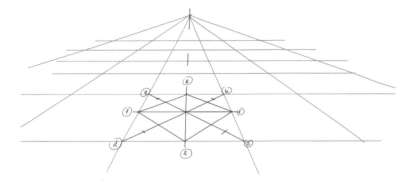

FIG 6.30 Ellipses.

Draw the ellipse, starting at the top, working your way around the interior of the shape, and touching the center marks on the diagonals. Some animators like to draw the curves so that they fall short of those marks, and some like to be right on the marks. As long as you get a nice clean sweep to your lines, anywhere within that range, center to slightly short, will serve you well. You're drawing this freehand, so be as accurate as possible and try to avoid pinching the arcs too much so you don't get points on your arcs (see Figure 6.31).

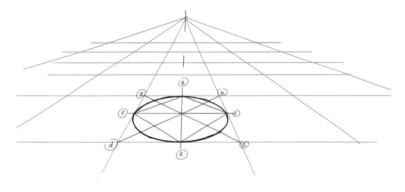

FIG 6.31 Ellipses.

Perspective plays a big part in effects animation and must be practiced and mastered. It will very likely be necessary in a great many effects problems you will come up against, and the better you know how to solve those problems, the easier it will be to get your animation right. Remember that your goal should always be to do it right the first time! Understanding perspective will help you accomplish that task. I would encourage you to draw freehand ellipses and circles so that you become more confident in your skills to be able to "eyeball it" whenever possible. But be able to lay down a grid for accuracy when it gets tricky to avoid mistakes.

CHAPTER 7

Water

Part 1: Ocean Waves

Water gives us life. Water flowing sparkling bright. Flowing and ebbing in the night.
Hearing that sound with such delight as I calmly drift to sleep tonight.

—*Cynthia Maressa*

This chapter will comprise many aspects under the heading of *water*. I will show you how I approach different effects problems and how you can work to solve them yourself. I encourage you to practice your own solutions to problems you encounter as you go out and sketch and by writing copious notes on your observations. Reading about how to do something is only the beginning of your learning process. Drawing and sketching from life is putting into practice what you read about and the best way I know of mastering your techniques. I will start with the broad movements and work down to the more detailed as we progress.

Let me begin first with ocean waves, swells, and currents. I like working things out by understanding the back story of the effects I animate—that is to say, how it may have started its life cycle before it got to where I start the animation. Ocean currents are affected mostly by the Earth's rotation and the gravitational pull of the moon as well as the sun, and for the most part they run more deeply under the surface of the water. Although the cycle of the ocean tides are an effect of the moon's gravitational pull, what is the cause of the waves on the surface of the oceans?

Waves are a transfer of energy from the air to the water surface. Wind moving over the surface of the ocean water (*friction*) actually transfers that energy to the water, causing waves or causing the water to ripple and grow to become waves that move up and down in a circular motion from the surface down to the depth of about half its wave length and back up again (see Figure 7.1).

FIG 7.1 Wind causes waves.

The energy (*inertia*) carries waves forward, eventually amassing to form swells that are more uniform. These swells are usually the result of storms out at sea and they can invariably travel great distances. A swell is more of a rolling-type action, with the familiar crest and trough measuring its overall height; depending on the wavelength that can sometimes be quite long (see Figure 7.2).

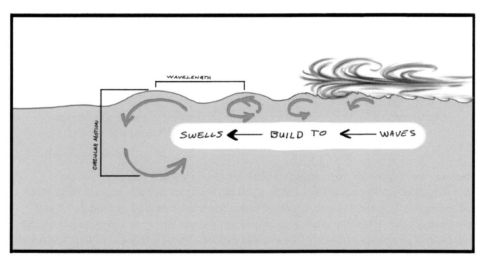

FIG 7.2 Waves build to swells.

The rolling action is evident in the movement that you see on a buoy out at sea. The circular motion of the swells heaves the buoy forward as the wave navigates through the buoy's position from trough to crest and back down to the trough, where it is upright again. Follow the progression of the illustrations of buoys numbered 1–9 to observe the action that occurs (see Figure 7.3).

I'm sure you've probably seen films of ships at sea in major storms, where the ship bobs up and down over giant swells that can loom at overwhelming heights and be separated by many feet apart from crest to crest, sometimes with vast troughs between them.

To animate swells or waves, we need to understand the principles of *follow-through* and *overlapping action*. Let's look at the "rope snake" example. A man holding a rope

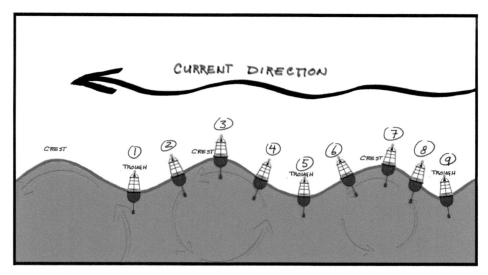

FIG 7.3 Swells.

moves his arm up and down in a quick action, flipping the rope forward away from him. Remember, *for every action there is an opposite and equal reaction*. That action transfers the energy to the rope, initiating a wave motion. The transfer of energy from arm to rope continues through the rope, moving beyond where the arm has stopped. *Inertia* then carries the action through the length of the rope. Such is the case with ocean swells (see Figure 7.4).

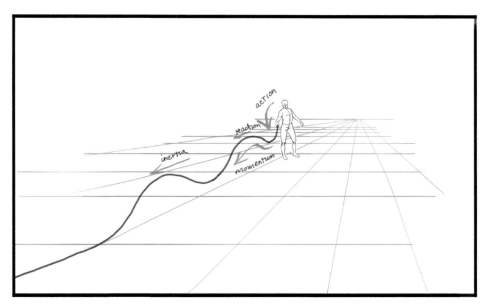

FIG 7.4 Overlap transfer of energy.

I've done a series of drawings showing examples of overlapping action that occurs as swelling waves travel over the surface of the ocean. I drew the waves with contouring lines on them not only to indicate the volume of the waves but also to show the direction in which they are traveling, over the crest and down to the trough of the waves. I use this numbering technique to help me keep track of the animation. It can become confusing sometimes when there are too many overlapping lines on the paper. Any technique you use to help you stay in control of your animation is acceptable. Just remember to erase those guidelines when you finalize your animation, usually at the assistant stage.

Track the action of the waves in Figures 7.5 through 7.11. Note that the action is very similar to the "snake" action from the rope example (Figure 7.4).

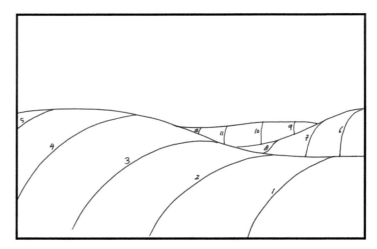

FIG **7.5** Swells 1.

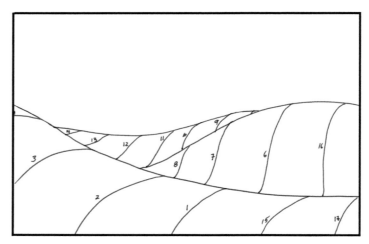

FIG **7.6** Swells 2.

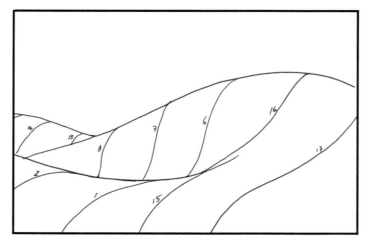

FIG **7.7** Swells 3.

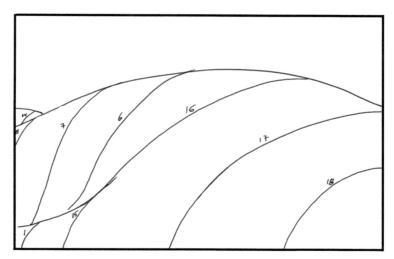

FIG 7.8 Swells 4.

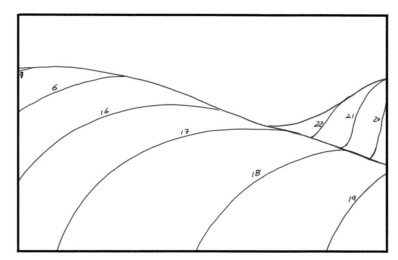

FIG 7.9 Swells 5.

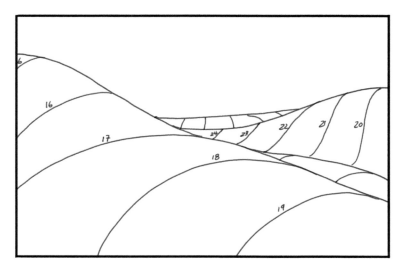

FIG 7.10 Swells 6.

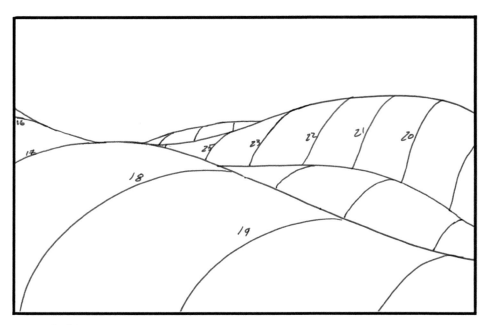

FIG **7.11** Swells 7.

Wind or a storm or even a shift in tectonic plates initiates the action, causing the surface of the water to swell and travel great distances, eventually terminating on land as waves or even a tsunami crashing onto a shoreline. The circular movement of water within a wave is slower in the deep waters of the ocean, causing the swells to have a more leisurely motion and giving the impression of a slow-moving mass, which is not always the case. These swells can move rapidly at times and with great force due to their great mass (see Figure 7.12).

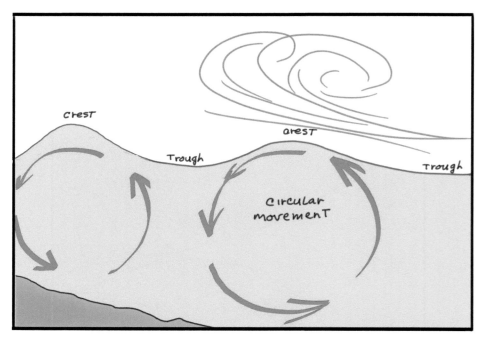

FIG **7.12** Circular movement.

As the swells get closer to shore and the water gets shallower, the waves begin to peak and eventually break, because the circular action causing the forward progress of the wave cannot maintain the height of the wave to complete its cycle. As the waves wash ashore onto the beach, the energy is finally disbursed (see Figure 7.13).

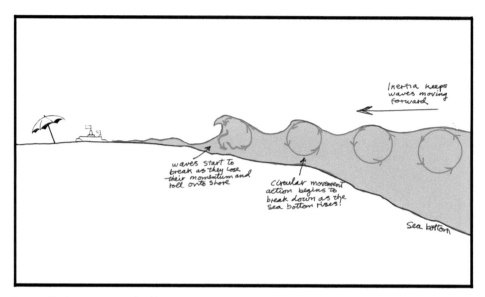

FIG 7.13 Circular wave movement breakdown.

As the waves reach the shoreline, they curl over and crash onto the beach in a burst of foam and misty spray. Their speed and momentum suddenly checked by the shore line, the waves wash ashore in a series of overlapping actions. The waves continually roll onto shore, while the spent waves begin receding back to the main body of water (see Figure 7.14).

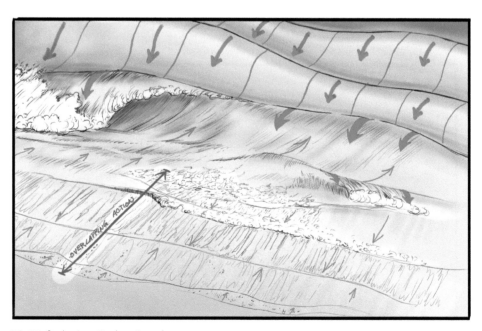

FIG 7.14 Overlapping action dynamics on shore.

Sheets of the spent waves slide back out and merge with the oncoming rush of new waves. These sheets of water and foam blend with the new waves as if they are being sucked up by the oncoming ones from below in a series of overlapping actions. The spent ones travel back to the main body at the same time as the new waves continue to crash on shore (see Figure 7.15).

FIG 7.15 Overlapping wave action on shore.

Let's look at the waves coming onto shore at eye level. For this we draw a perspective grid, as we will need this to help with timing the distant swells in scale with the closer ones. Even though there will be the same number of inbetween drawings for the closer waves and those further away, note that they will be spaced differently. Wave 1 will travel the distance from a to b, Wave 2 from b to c, and Wave 3 from c to d. The spacing between Waves 1, 2, 3, and 4 is proportionately the same distance using the perspective grid, but the waves will travel at different speeds due to our viewing angle (see Figure 7.16).

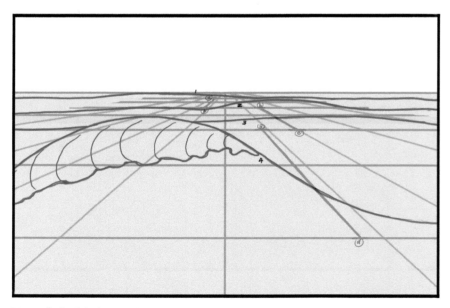

FIG 7.16 Scaling timing in perspective.

The distant waves are more bunched together but cover the same distance, according to the perspective grid, as the closer ones. They look like they aren't moving as fast as the foreground ones due to the distant and shallow viewing angle. The timing chart on the right indicates the number of drawings that will be required between Wave 3 and Wave 4 and the spacing of the drawings. Here, Drawing 7 will be our breakdown drawing, or the middle drawing, while the others will be spaced according to how they are indicated on the chart. I've illustrated them in Figure 7.17.

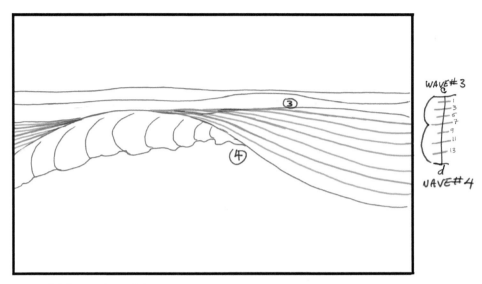

FIG 7.17 Scale foreground waves timing.

I've indicated the same in Figures 7.18 and 7.19 as well. The waves are all evenly timed, meaning that each travels in the same amount of time from Wave 1 to Wave 2 as Wave 2 to Wave 3 and Wave 3 to Wave 4.

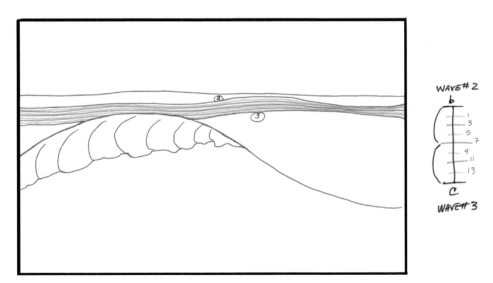

FIG 7.18 Scale midground waves timing.

While this timing may work fine, I like to vary it a bit just to accentuate the perspective a bit more and give the scene a greater sense of scale and mass. You can do this by simply adding more inbetween drawings. However, when you do that, make sure that you adjust

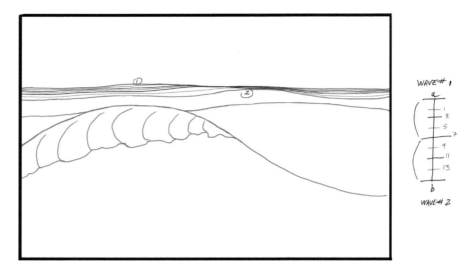

FIG 7.19 Scaling background waves timing.

the middle ground waves as well, so that you maintain a good scale progression from distant to foreground. This can be achieved by adding drawings to the first few drawings between Wave 2 and Wave 3. Note the charts in Figure 7.20. The original chart appears in Figure 7.19; note where I've added the extra drawings (inbetweens) to slow down Wave 1. I added the extra drawings to Wave 2 at the beginning of the chart, going into Wave 3; the slow out of Wave 2 is in order to transition more smoothly from Wave 1 to Wave 2. This technique ensures that there is no sudden timing jerk from Wave 1 to Wave 2 as they blend into one another.

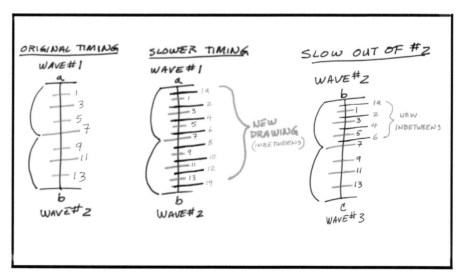

FIG 7.20 Timing charts.

Variations on your timing will take practice and trial and error to perfect and will make a world of difference to your animation. *So, practice, practice, practice!*

Part 2: Large Splashes

Roll on deep and dark blue ocean, roll

—Lord Byron

When I animate or draw water, I usually use a blue pencil. This is a psychological approach that I learned from Ed Aardall, my first mentor in animating effects, and it just stuck with me. I think a lot of effects animators probably use this approach. This is how I learned and I'm just passing it on. When you animate water, use a blue colored pencil. For fire, use a red one; brown for mud, and so on. Graphite is for the final cleaned-up animation, but color pencils for roughs work best for me. Now that it is commonplace to use a stylus on a tablet, anything goes, anyway! Of course, whatever is comfortable for your approach is the best way for you.

When we understand the nitty-gritty of what actually happens when an object hits a body of water, we can then work out the logistics of our designs much more easily. Ask yourself, is the water deep or shallow? Are there other objects in the water that may deflect the object hitting the water? Is the object that is hitting the water large or small? Irregularly shaped or smooth? Will the object hit at an oblique angle or perpendicular to the surface? Is the perspective grid in place in the layout or must I draw one so that my ellipses can work better with the background?

The crown or splash that occurs can take on a variety of shapes, but the dynamics of splashes are fairly similar. Object hits water; water is displaced, causing the splash; water from the splash radiates out and upward from the impact area. As the water shoots up, its elasticity allows it to stretch and get thinner until it starts to tear; the surface tension of the water can only maintain its shape for so long before separating into smaller shapes and droplets. These tears separate the portions of the splash water. The uppermost tears away, forming sheets of spray and droplets that travel in an arc trajectory radiating away from the impact point at the center. That spray and droplets will eventually complete their arcs and land back in the water some distance from the impact center. Depending on the speed and mass of the rock, the perimeter around the splash can be great or small.

What exactly happens when, let's say, a rock is dropped into a body of water? Let's say it's a pretty good-sized rock falling straight down. First the water is displaced. It has to go somewhere! The rock just replaced the space it occupied in the main body of water when it entered the realm of the liquid, spraying water in all directions. For the purpose of simplicity, I will illustrate this with the water surface at eye level, with a cutout of a splash. The rock displaces the water as it sinks (Figure 7.21).

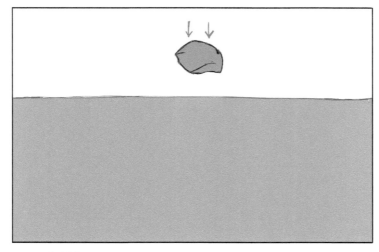

FIG 7.21 Rock falling into water.

It leaves an air pocket trailing behind it. This air pocket is important for a number of reasons, as you will see (see Figures 7.22 and 7.23).

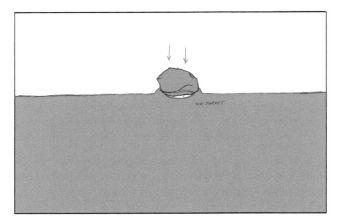

FIG 7.22 Rock displacing water.

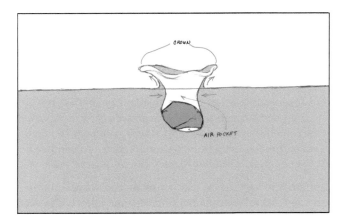

FIG 7.23 Rock creates air pocket.

The air pocket collapses onto itself (see Figures 7.24 and 7.25).

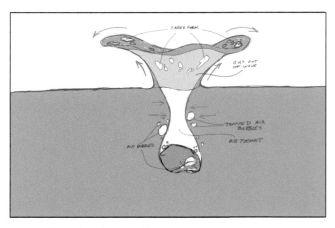

FIG 7.24 Water collapses back on itself.

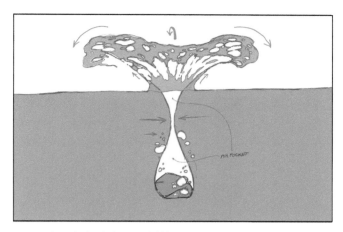

FIG 7.25 Air pocket breaks down into bubbles.

The walls of the air pockets collapse, causing a secondary splash to shoot up within the radius of the initial displacement crown (splash) (see Figures 7.26 and 7.27).

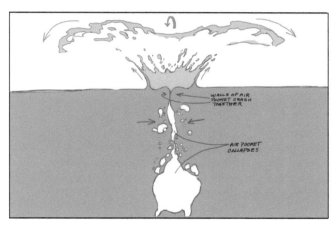

FIG 7.26 Collapse pushes water upward.

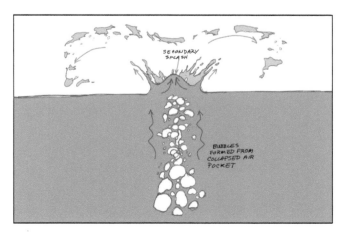

FIG 7.27 Secondary splash occurs.

As the rock sinks to the bottom, it drags some of that air pocket along with it, which ends up collapsing into a variety of bubbles that float to the surface, pushing water up and out (more overlapping action!) and resulting in the secondary splash.

The lower part of the splash crown that has torn away from the upper portion of the splash simply collapses smoothly back down into the main body of water as a series of ripples, radiating out away from the splash (see Figure 7.28).

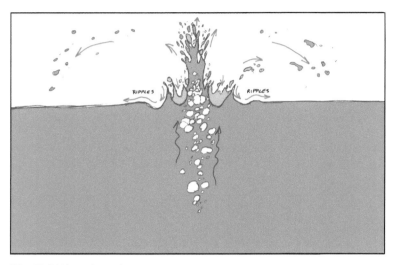

FIG 7.28 Bubble travel upward.

Here are a series of splash designs determined by different angles of impact. The first is an oblique angle. Again, my perspective grid helps me out in achieving an accurate angle-to-background blend. First I rough out my perspective. Then I rough out the angle of trajectory and ellipses indicating the radius and the direction in which I believe the splash will spread from the impact point before drawing the actual splash (see Figures 7.29 and 7.30).

Here are some examples of splashes from a variety of angles of objects striking the water surface (see Figure 7.31).

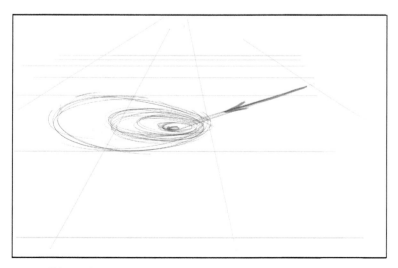

FIG 7.29 Oblique angle perspective.

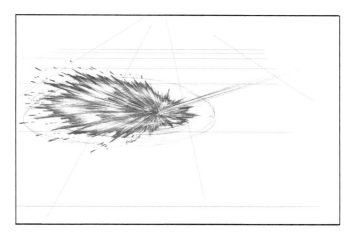

FIG 7.30 Design splash.

FIG 7.31 Splash samples.

I'm including some simplified splash designs with only the general shapes of the splashes. It's always a good idea to practice simplifying the shapes the splashes will take during the course of your animation. Simplicity is always the best course to take when animating. This will assure you of the correct proportions and dynamics of the design before you start your animation (see Figure 7.32).

FIG 7.32 Simplified designs.

Part 3: Skipping Stones

Skipping a stone across a lake requires a good arm and practice so you're consistent at throwing that stone in relatively the same angle as it strikes the water. The goal is to throw it with enough force so that it "slaps" and skims over the surface of the water just enough to then continue arcing over the water again to its next contact point, without it hitting the water at such an angle that it sinks. It needs to skip over the water and "slap" at it again and again for as long and as many strikes as possible. Here's a progression of the skipping stone action in Figures 7.33 and 7.34. Note that when the stone strikes the water the splashing occurs to either side from the direction that the stone is traveling. As the stone skips ahead, a small trail of water clings to it.

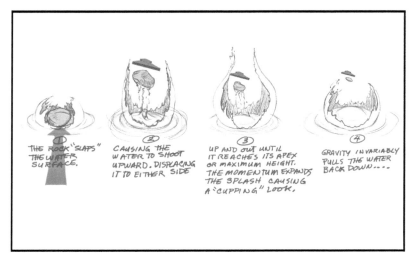

FIG 7.33 Skipping stone.

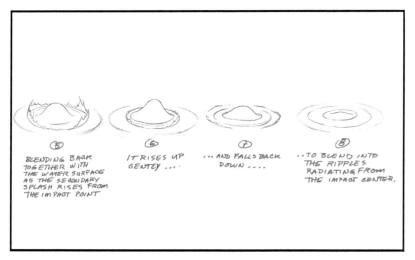

FIG 7.34 Secondary splash settling.

The splash actually causes a cupping effect as it forms. The look is further accentuated as the splash settles back to the water surface. The secondary splash is not as pronounced as it would be had the stone plunged directly into the water. Because it only skimmed over the surface the secondary slash is more of a convex dimple that rises, then blends back down, rippling out from the center of the impact.

More samples of the effect of skipping stones from a different angle (see Figure 7.35).

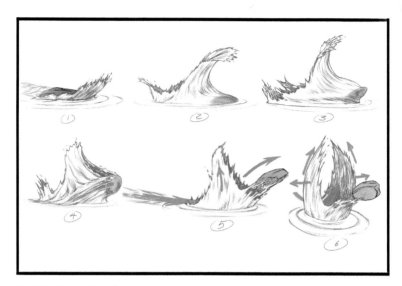

FIG 7.35 Skipping stone effect.

Here are some more preliminary sketches I made while researching the skipping stones reference. These were made while watching film reference and some feeble attempts on my part to skip stones on a calm ocean surface. This exercise was fun but left me with a sore shoulder! (see Figures 7.36 and 7.37).

FIG 7.36 Skipping stones 1.

FIG 7.37 Skipping stones 2.

Part 4: Overlap, Follow-Through, and Drag

This example of dragging an oar through water is to illustrate how overlap, follow-through, and drag work. The oar cleaves the water (1) with a little bit of splash in both direction. As the oar is drawn back to propel the boat forward, it forces the water to swell ahead of it (2) until the oar reaches its maximum distance and is lifted out of the water (3) so the oarsman can repeat the action. As the oar is lifted up and out to sweep (4) forward for the next stroke, water clings to the oar and drips off (*drag*) of it in an arc as it follows the path (*follow-through*) (5) being described in the air by the oar, while a greater portion of the dripping water cascades back into the main body of water (*overlapping action*). The drips coming off of the oar will continue to travel forward even after the oar has plunged into the water as they continue to follow the arc (see Figure 7.38).

FIG 7.38 Overlap, follow-through, and drag.

Part 5: Rain Cycle

I bring fresh showers for the thirsty flowers

—Percy Bysshe Shelley

When setting up a rain cycle, use at least three levels of rain animation. When animating a rain cycle, each raindrop must travel from the top of the frame to the bottom as in Figure 7. 39. Animate each drop (1–11) and then expose the drop animation (1–11 and then back to 1). Repeat the cycle as many times as needed for the length of the scene.

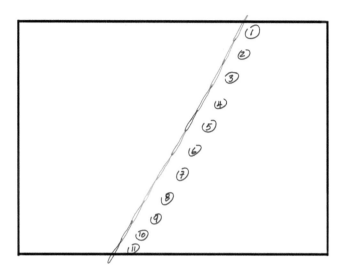

FIG 7.39 Raindrop spacing.

Stagger the rain levels and make sure the drops don't follow the same path and overlap onto other drops on different levels (see Figures 7.40 through 7.42).

FIG 7.40 Raindrop pattern level 1.

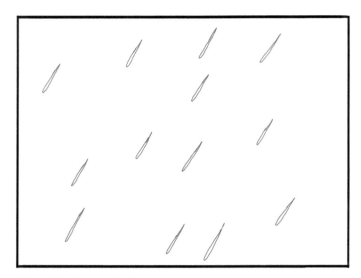

FIG 7.41 Raindrop pattern level 2.

FIG 7.42 Raindrop pattern level 3.

During a rain shower, the puddles that form in depressions have bubbles constantly forming and popping as the raindrops hit. How does this happen? Raindrops hit the standing water with such force and speed that, as the splash occurs, the crown closes up and captures air inside. Here is the sequence of events (see Figure 7.43).

This happens rather quickly, and the surface tension is so delicate that it may give way at any moment, causing the bubble to pop (see Figure 7.44).

In the next examples, I illustrate five possible raindrop hits. As you can see, they are very simple pieces of animation lasting anywhere from four to seven frame cycles. These can be exposed over and over, one after the other, as in Figure 7.49 and will look like constant rain hitting the ground (see Figures 7.45 through 7.47).

FIG 7.43 Bubbles form.

FIG 7.44 Bubble popping.

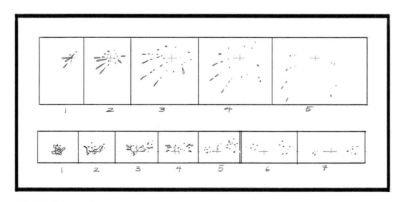

FIG 7.45 Raindrop hits 1.

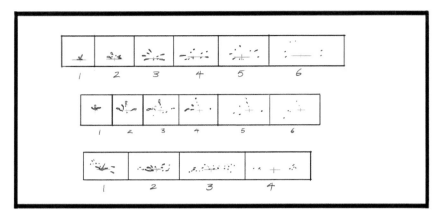

FIG 7.46 Raindrop hits 2.

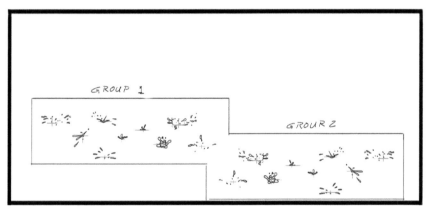

FIG 7.47 Raindrop hits 3.

These are pieces of animation that I would animate and compile in a variety of groups. I would then arrange the groupings within my field on the ground plane. Each drop represented one of my animated raindrop cycles as many times as was needed to cover the ground to my satisfaction. The red hash marks assured me of the correct position of each raindrop cycle, marking the center of the hit (see Figure 7.48).

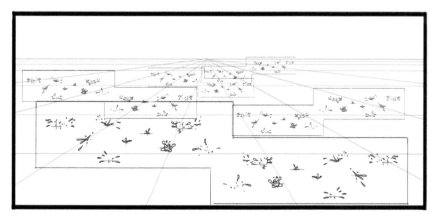

FIG 7.48 Raindrop hits reuse pattern.

I would then copy and reduce in scale and arrange those further back in the background in perspective as many times as needed to cover the entire ground plane in the scene and cycle the animation for the duration of the scene (see Figure 7.49).

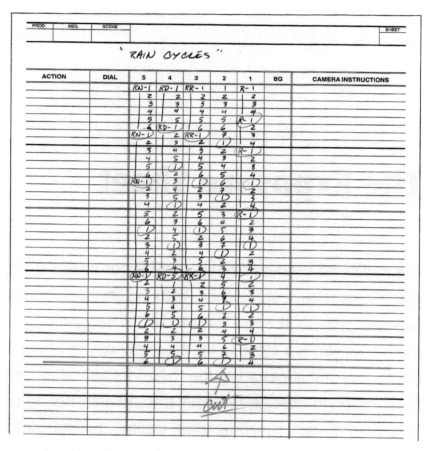

FIG 7.49 Rain cycle exposed on exposure sheet.

Part 6: Bubbles

Design the bubble effect you will be animating, if necessary with color separations (separate levels) that will comprise each bubble for the desired effect (see Figure 7.50).

FIG 7.50 Bubble design.

Now you will need to distinguish the separate levels—the main body of the bubble and the highlight levels (see Figures 7.51 through 7.53).

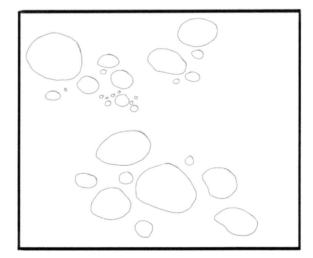

FIG 7.51 Bubble main bodies.

All these levels will get painted black in the computer ink and paint program in the color models department (see Figures 7.54 through 7.56).

While in the color model department, each of these levels receives a specific color and diffusion or blur, according to the specifications of the art director. All the levels are then composited together and final adjustments are made with the desired opacity for the final compositing into the scene.

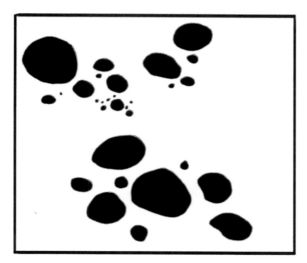

FIG 7.52 Painted bubbles.

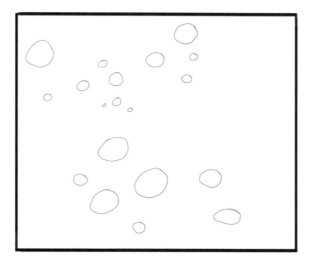

FIG 7.53 Bubble cores.

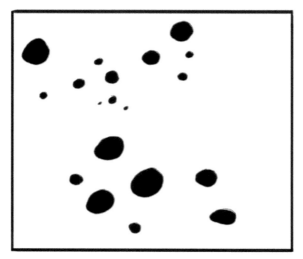

FIG 7.54 Bubble cores painted.

FIG 7.55 Small bubbles.

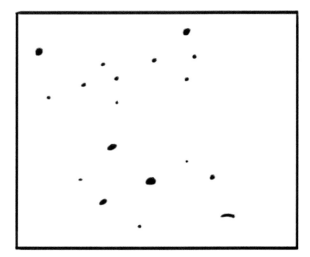

FIG 7.56 Small bubbles painted.

In years gone by, each of these steps were done in the ink and paint department, where each bubble was inked onto a celluloid sheet and painted the necessary colors. The artwork would then go to the camera department, where each level would be shot on separate film strips. The film strips would later be composited with the required diffusion, blur, and opacity. But before the final compositing, the cameraman would need to shoot a series of "wedges," or exposure tests, to determine the correct exposure needed.

Bubbles, animated rising underwater, would never travel in a straight line. First, determine the path you wish the bubbles to travel (see Figure 7.57).

Roughly animate a single bubble and shoot a pencil test to see if it is traveling the way you want it to and at the speed you think is appropriate (see Figure 7.58).

Once this is done, go back to the beginning frame and roughly animate the rest of your bubbles following the lead of your test bubble. Note that bubbles underwater are not perfectly round and will change their shape slightly as they animate. The changes should not be great or rapid as they morph from one shape to another, but they do so in a sluggish fashion so as not to make them look as if they are popping (see Figure 7.59).

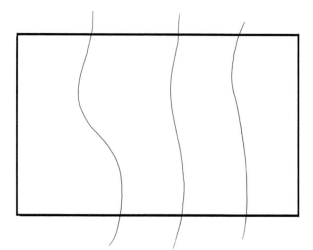

FIG 7.57 Bubble animation path of action.

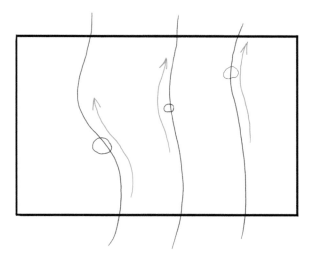

FIG 7.58 Bubble animation timing.

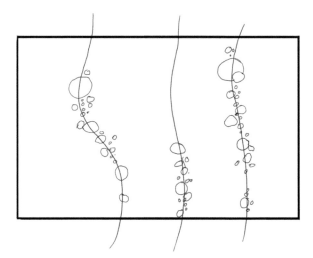

FIG 7.59 Bubble animation patterns.

If you are animating on twos (one drawing exposed on every other frame of film, every two frames), the spacing of the drawings needs to be the height of the bubbles' diameter. That means that the smaller bubbles will by necessity rise slower that the larger ones (see Example 1 in Figure 7.60). If you're animating on ones (each drawing exposed on every frame of film), then the bubbles will need to overlap (see Example 2). If you animate a group of bubbles together on twos, then the entire group has to travel as one unit, with overlapping action and follow-through as you animate following the path you set for yourself (see Example 3).

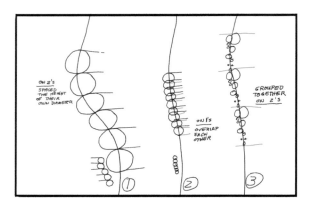

FIG 7.60 Bubble animation spacing.

Here is an example showing the difference in exposing animation on ones and twos on an exposure sheet. Note that when animating on twos the numbering follows the pattern 1, 3, 5, 7, 9, 11, 13, and so on. The reason for this is simple. If you need to slow something down or smooth out an action, you can simply go to the area that needs the adjustment and insert new drawings. Let's say we need to smooth out the action between Drawings 1, 3, and 5. We then add Drawings 2 and 4 and solve the problem area (see Figure 7.61).

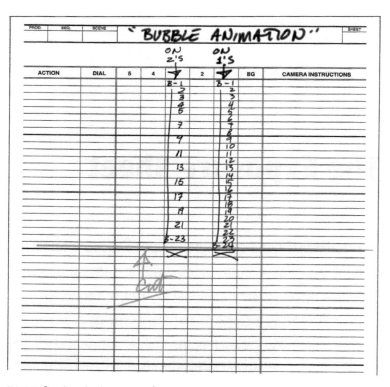

FIG 7.61 Exposing animation on ones and twos.

Part 7: Geysers

Geysers are streams of superheated water under great pressure. Its initial gush shoots upward and may settle back down, then back up again with greater force until it eventually reaches its maximum height. The scale it achieves can vary depending on the force behind it. It's possible for it to shoot up to 100 feet or more like Old Faithful or as high as 3–5 sputtering feet (see Figure 7.62).

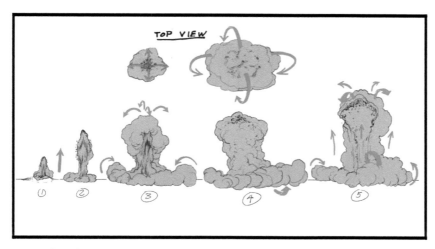

FIG 7.62 Geyser dynamics.

The geyser can be animated as several separate levels. The jet spray is the core of the overall effect. The jet level can spray upward, sputtering in numerous rapid convulsions comparable to percolating coffee (geyser image 1 in Figure 7.63). The jet sprays up and eventually fans out, dispersing into a fine mist. A level of steam or mist can follow the jet, surrounding it as it climbs upward, while another level of mist can waft upward and away from the source (geyser image 2 in Figure 7.63).

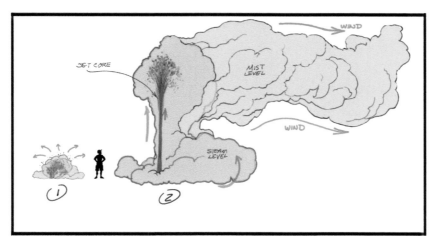

FIG 7.63 Geyser breakdown of elements.

The jet core level would be the bottommost level that would be animated under the steam and mist levels. The mist is just cooled-off steam that will be carried off by the wind, drifting away from the superheated source jet core, cooling as it does, and becoming heavier the more it cools. Some of the mist may evaporate into the atmosphere; most will settle back to earth as gravity pulls the heavy water vapor back down, soaking the surrounding landscape.

The geyser can last a matter of a few seconds or possibly much longer, pulsing up and down as the heated liquid continually blasts upward. The geyser can be animated in several separate levels. The jet spray can be the core of the overall effect. A level of steam or mist can follow the jet, surrounding it as it climbs upward, while another level of mist can waft upward and away from the source. The jet and the steam surrounding it can be animated as a cycle once it reaches its maximum height, and the wafting mist can be animated straight ahead, drifting slowly away (see Figure 7.64).

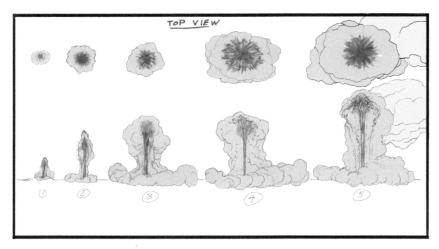

FIG 7.64 Geyser top and side views.

Part 8: Waterfalls

The layout department will present you with a scene having an interesting perspective with a design for the effect to start you out. Spend some time studying the scene before you put pencil to paper and try to imagine not only what the water looks like going over the edge but also the tremendous rumble that the water makes as it falls to the valley below. This visualization in your mind's eye will help you develop the timing in the animation and will be time well spent in any animation you do (see Figure 7.65).

FIG 7.65 Waterfall layout.

Before you start animating, you may want to do something that will help you define your design and animation a bit more. When dealing with large-scale waterfall effects, you will want to use multiple levels to get a sense of depth of focus by blurring the furthest level away from camera when the focus of the scene is close to the camera or blurring the closest levels and sharpening the focus on the back levels when the focus of the scene is there. The best and easiest way for you to do that, of course, is to use multiple levels on your waterfalls as well as separate levels in your construction of your waterfall. So, a level for the main body of the falls, a separate level for whitewater/foam, a level for trickling water in some areas for contrast to the mass and volume of your main foreground effect, and of course a separate mist level.

First look at the layout without the waterfall elements, just the bare landscape (see Figure 7.66).

FIG 7.66 Waterfall layout only.

If you feel that you can spice up the design of the water a bit more than what is on the layout, then you can start by first adding something to the layout on a separate level for your sole benefit—nothing that can be seen but just to act as a guide for you to animate to. This will help you to animate highs and lows in the water level or obstructions that you can use as areas where you can animate a splash or whitewater dips or peaks to create silhouettes that are a bit more interesting (see Figure 7.67).

FIG 7.67 Waterfall layout with added rocks.

Now do the initial design for your waterfall effect, what it will look like in the foreground and in the distant background if necessary (see Figure 7.68).

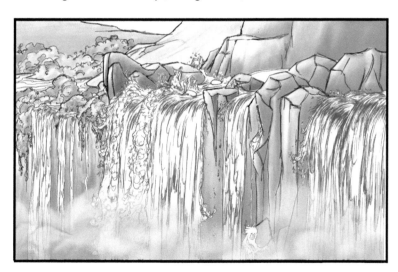

FIG 7.68 Waterfall with animation design.

The waterfall in the background does not need to be as detailed as your foreground, so simplify your design for that effect and animate it as a separate level (see Figure 7.69).

Waterfalls can usually be animated as cycle animation, meaning that you can animate a minimum number of drawings to complete the waterfall, animating from top to bottom. Use the animation over and over again a number of times, depending on the length of your scene by cycling those drawings from first to last, then back to the first or one in the middle, as long as it transitions smoothly from one to the other.

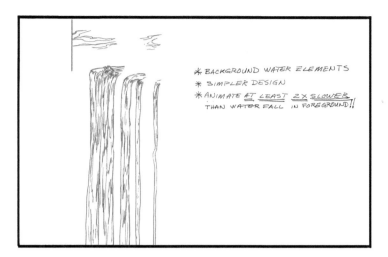

FIG 7.69 Waterfall: distant animation.

When I animate a waterfall, especially if the effect is close to the camera and in focus in a particularly long scene, I animate the water cycling with at least two or three transitioning cycles. This eliminates the obvious pulsing that develops when the same drawings are used over and over again in a particularly long scene, which may become distracting. For the purpose of simplification, in this example I'm animating a 16-frame cycle. The animation is from Frame 1 to Frame 13, using Frames 13 and 1 to make my transitional inbetween animation drawing (Frame 15) (see Figure 7.70).

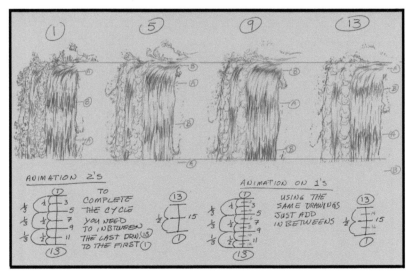

FIG 7.70 Waterfall animation cycles.

Note that I'm numbering my drawings using odd numbers. This, of course, is for the eventuality that I may need to make inbetween drawings to lengthen the animation from Drawings 1 through 15 back to 1 to an alternative 1 through 16 only on twos. Another alternative would be to simply smooth out the animation and put them on ones. See Figure 7.71 for variations on exposing the waterfall animation.

The mist levels are separate levels for the foreground and background effect. The mist in the background would show only a little movement and would require as few as four drawings that would cycle (see Figure 7.72).

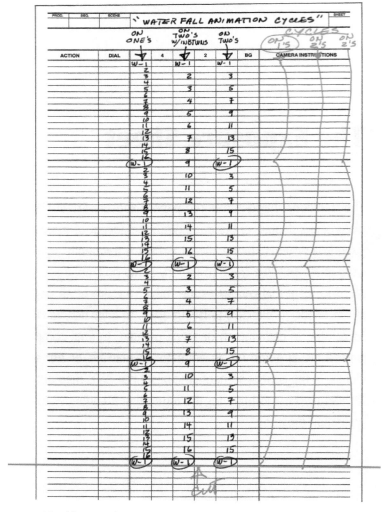

FIG 7.71 Waterfall exposure sheet.

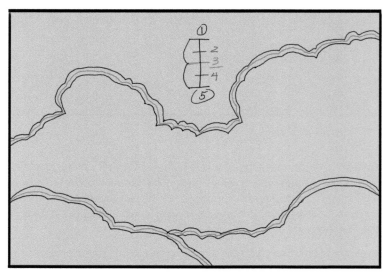

FIG 7.72 Mist cycles.

After animating the cycle, I would expose the drawings with a 30%–40% opacity and a strong blur to simulate my key drawing (see Figure 7.68). I cycle those drawings on my exposure sheet and give the camera department directions for how to expose them, as well as shooting them with four-frame cross dissolves on the cycle (1 through 5 and back to 1) (see Figure 7.73).

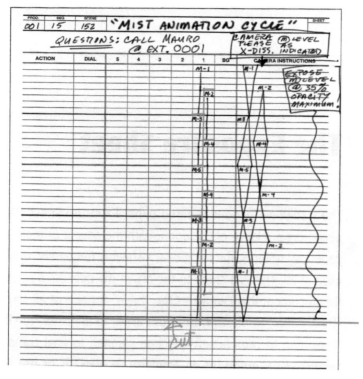

FIG 7.73 Mist cycles exposure sheet.

My final image for waterfalls is just a simplification pass on the waterfall animation. I eliminated the multiple sketchy line and used whole shapes as a contrasting design to the more complex ones (see Figure 7.74). When pressed for time on the neverending deadlines we have on productions, it's always best to have an alternative design and a way to simplify the effect.

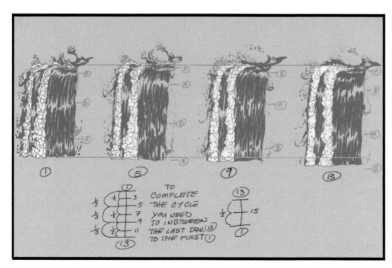

FIG 7.74 Waterfall: simpler animation design.

Part 9: Rivers

Rivers can run deep or shallow; they can be turbulent rapids with classifications of difficulty to navigate on with rafts or kayaks or, like the mighty Mississippi, flow ponderously, in places looking like they are hardly moving because of their vast expanse. A waterway like that may require only a reflection on its surface to animate and give it a sense of movement—a simple eight-frame cycle on twos, or 1, 3, 5, and 7 (see the chart in Figure 7.75). The cycle would start with Drawings 1 through 5, with Drawing 3 as the breakdown drawing between those numbers, then in-between Drawings 5 to 1 to get Drawing 7 to complete the cycle. You could also add inbetween drawing throughout the cycle and get a cycle on ones, or 1, 2, 3, 4, 5, 6, 7, and 8, for a more fluid action (see Figures 7.75 through 7.78).

FIG 7.75 River effects animation with timing charts.

FIG 7.76 River effects animation 1.

A stream or a brook can flow with a calming trickling or bubbling sound and with a clarity in the water that allows you to view the rocky bottom, with glimpses of fish swimming lazily about. Animating simple shapes along the banks of the waterway and maybe an occasional ripple off center of the body of water, where a rock or grass or a branch may protrude, would suffice to show the action of the surface water animation in these cases (see Figure 7.79).

Handle the ripples as overlapping shapes that are constantly flowing downstream. Keep the speed of the animation appropriate to the volume of water. Wide waterways will more than likely move more slowly than narrow passages, where the flow of water will pick up speed (see Figure 7.80).

FIG 7.77 River effects animation 2.

FIG 7.78 River effects animation 3.

FIG 7.79 River ripple animation.

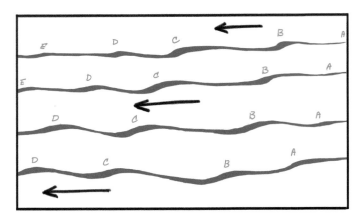

FIG 7.80 Ripple flow progression.

A river will cut through the landscape, flowing with the grade of the land, slowly in wide areas and picking up speed as it flows through narrow channels. It may converge with other rivers on its journey toward the sea, or it may suddenly go underground and disappear. As it flows over and around obstacles like rocks in its path, it may "pillow" or swell behind the rock and eventually spill around it, where it may be subjected to turbulence and cause whitewater in the spillways or suddenly settle into an eddy, a calm spot in front of the rock downstream (see Figures 7.81 and 7.82).

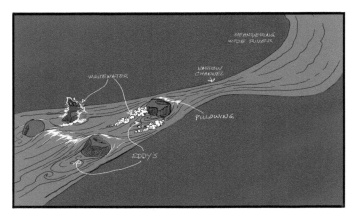

FIG 7.81 Ripple flow variations 1.

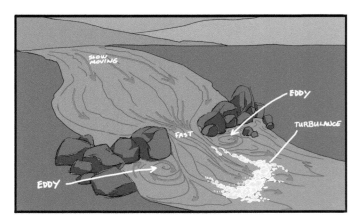

FIG 7.82 Ripple flow variations 2.

In the next examples, I illustrate water flowing in a river as it plunges into a hollow behind a large rock. Here, the water piles up as it tries to flow over the top of the rock but only manages to pillow on the back of the rock, spilling over the sides with a turbulent force that causes whitewater to erupt as it flows around the rock. On the downstream side of the rock, an eddy of calmer water forms as water rushes past the rock on both sides (Figure 7.83).

FIG 7.83 Pillowing and white water.

For the next illustration, I separate the main body of the river water layer, indicating the action as the water cascades into the hollow behind the rock and spills around it (see Figure 7.84).

FIG 7.84 River flow action.

Next, I add the foam or whitewater in the areas appropriate for it—where the water crashes into the hollow, creating turbulence, and around the areas where the water rushes around the rock and agitates the convergence of the spillage (see Figure 7.85).

Another example of pillowing action happening is when the rapids are so violent that there's no eddy forming on the downstream side of the rock but only violently foaming whitewater action. There is a piling up of water behind the rock formation, and the water spilling over and around the rocks is a straight drop that only creates turbulence and foaming action (see Figure 7.86).

Here's an example of a river falls where there is a sudden drop in its course. I first make a drawing or a key of what it looks like, then break down the levels or the different layers that I think I'll need to make the animation as economically as I can and still have a great-looking animated effect (see Figure 7.87).

FIG 7.85 Turbulen foam level.

FIG 7.86 White water river.

FIG 7.87 River spillway.

My next step is to determine the bottom-most level that works on top of the background but under all the other levels, including any characters in the setup. This will be the surface of the river rushing downstream. I could animate this level simply and on a cycle that could be repeated over the length of the scene (see Figure 7.88).

My next level would be the whitewater levels. These I would animate separately in as many levels as I would need to cover the bottom level of the river surface (see Figure 7.89).

FIG 7.88 Bottom water level.

FIG 7.89 White water levels.

The levels would be exposed, with the bottom-most level (1) at the very bottom and the others exposed, layering one atop the other—Level 2 on top of Level 1, Level 3 on top of Level 2, Level 4 on top of Level 3. Each level slightly overlaps the other so as not to have gaps between them as they are animating (see Figure 7.90).

FIG 7.90 Multilevel breakdown.

To overlap these two bottom levels as they transition from water to foam, I would animate a level that covers where they overlap each other. This level would still be exposed under the character (the bear). This level could be painted dark to mimic a shallow depth where the water spills over the edge or light as a highlight level (see Figure 7.91).

FIG 7.91 Overlapping highlight level.

The next effects level would be exposed on top of the character as it would represent the turbulent foaming water formed by the force of the river water clashing against the bear (see Figure 7.92).

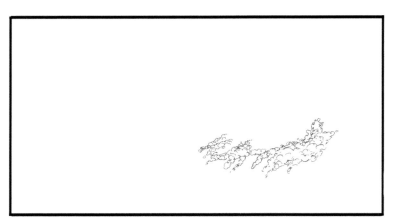

FIG 7.92 Foam level.

The final effect left to do would be the water falling off the unfortunate fish leaping out of the water (see Figure 7.93).

FIG 7.93 Water trailing behind fish.

CHAPTER 8

Fire

From a little spark may burst a flame!

—Dante Aligheri

Fire is the visual effect of combustion. It's an energy source humans have used for thousands of years. Humans have used and controlled it for cooking food, warming themselves through cold winters, and lighting their way on dark and foreboding nights. So what exactly is fire? Fire is a chemical reaction, the ignition of a fuel source such as wood and oxygen, creating heat and light not to mention smoke until the fuel is consumed. Humans probably adapted fire that they discovered from a natural occurrence, such as a lightning strike setting a fire, and were attracted to it for use against the elements. They used it for cooking and lighting their dwellings and later learned to create fire by accident, more than likely by the use of *friction*. The rapid rubbing together of two objects, such as wood, creates a heated surface that eventually smolders and, with oxygen from the air or from blowing on the smoldering embers, ignites into fire. No one will ever truly know how fire came to be discovered, but the fact that it has brought mankind great benefits through the ages is certain.

Humans have been lucky enough to be able to create fire much more easily than our early ancestors, since the early 1800s when matches were first developed. But how, you ask? Matches are a mixture of chemicals: red phosphorus, sulfur, and potassium chlorate. Striking the match head on a surface creates friction, which generates heat, igniting the phosphorus and in turn breaking down the chlorate, which generates oxygen to feed the fuel (sulfur) creating the fire. Now, aren't you glad you asked?

I highly recommend you research live-action film of fire, as well as still images. Do this enough and you will retain and recall how fire moves and acts under different conditions. Different scale fires move at different timings. Fire will also flare left and right in reaction to outside forces such as wind.

Let's start with the sequence of events from a match strike. Once ignited, the reaction of the chemicals sputters and may flicker and flare up and down rapidly and eventually settle to a fully formed flame. I would recommend that this effect be animated on ones and straight ahead. The sputtering flare-ups are fairly violent as they ignite and erratic in their action— that's why straight-ahead animation would work best here. Don't try to animate pose to pose and then do inbetweens for this effect. This would only make the animation look stiff and unnatural. A more random sputtering or helter-skelter action is appropriate in this case. It's also very important that when animating the action of dragging the matchstick across a surface, you make sure to follow a clear and smooth arc of action (see Figure 8.1). I would recommend animating the matchstick first and then "rolling" through your animation (see Figure 8.2) and confirming a smooth arc and path of action of the matchstick before you animate the flames.

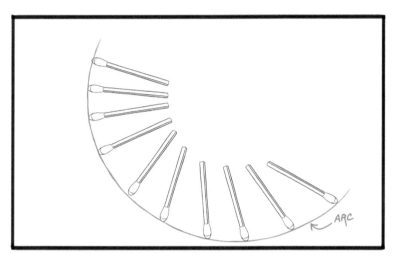

FIG 8.1 Match strike—arc.

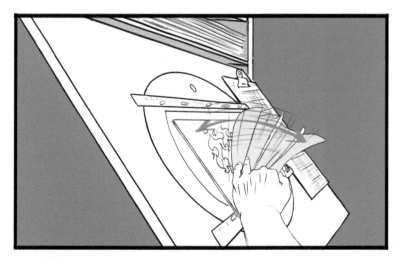

FIG 8.2 Rolling animation drawings.

You don't want the match animation to wobble around as you drag it and on the follow-through on your action (see Figure 8.3). This is not an acceptable arc! It flounders about and would impede the forward action of the animation.

FIG 8.3 Match strike—bad arc.

A smooth arc in your animation makes for a clear and confident piece of animation (see Figure 8.4).

FIG 8.4 Match strike—smooth arc.

Once the action is completed, you can follow the action that the hand holding it makes. It may be a smooth, confident motion to light a candle or a frightened, shaking hand trying to light a candle.

Once you strike a match and create fire on the end of that stick, you get the other product of combustion—smoke. Smoke is the tiny, solid, unburned particles of carbon and ash that are jettisoned from a fire. Smoke will bloom and expand from the fire source rapidly (see Figure 8.5).

As the fuel is burned away and the flame is extinguished, the smoke will fade away, trailing off from the final embers on the matchstick. The smoke blossoms out and up, contracting as it rises and then expanding. I'm using overlapping shapes for the expanding and contracting

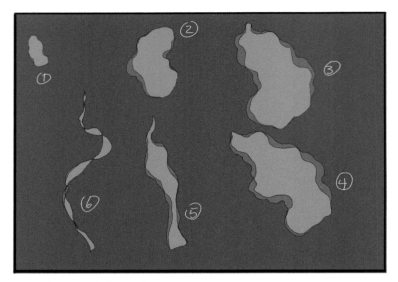

FIG 8.5 Separated smoke from match.

motion, with some added color separations to give the smoke a bit more body and a bit of interest as it animates in Figure 8.6.

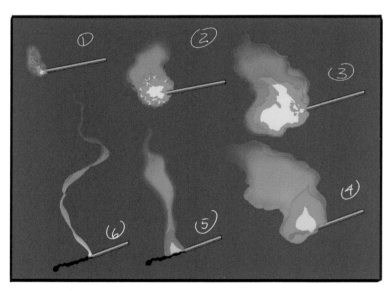

FIG 8.6 Match flame with smoke.

Animation of overlapping shapes is accomplished by animating the smoke by "snaking" the silhouette upward. I indicate a method to follow the shapes moving up in Figure 8.7.

By following some high and low points on the line of the silhouette and identifying them with some marks, letters, or numbers, you can keep track of the animation and make sure the shapes continue to move in the direction you intend (see Figure 8.8).

I would probably animate this smoke as straight-ahead animation, following the match and flame animation. Once the animation is complete, blur and opacity would be employed to add to the effect, both to the flame and the smoke (see Figure 8.6).

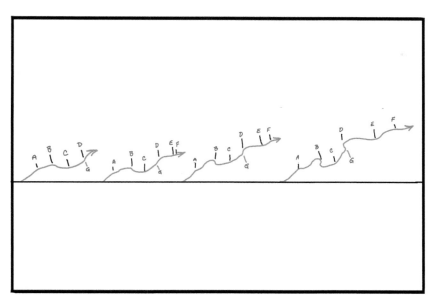

FIG 8.7 Tracking smoke shapes 1.

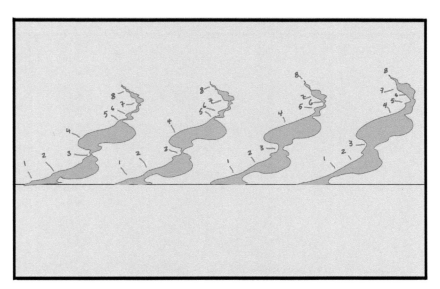

FIG 8.8 Tracking smoke shapes 2.

A candle flame has very little movement except when disturbed or when being carried around. The candle flame moves very subtly when it's in a stationary position, moving only slightly vertically and laterally. The animation timing charts in the illustration indicate the cycling of the animation: Drawings 1 through 11 and then back to Drawing 1, with 13 being the drawing that links the cycle. It cycles or loops all the animation for as long as you need to run it (see Figure 8.9).

Once the animation of the candle is completed, go to the final phase in the process: the compositing of the element for final color. Here is an example of how I would treat the candle for a production. It would involve multiple passes of the same element. On the first pass, I would use the line drawing (A) of the candle and slightly blur it (B). On the second pass, I would take the painted candle (C) and apply a slight blur to that as well (D). On the third pass, the painted candle element (C) would be used again by giving it a large blur (E) to be

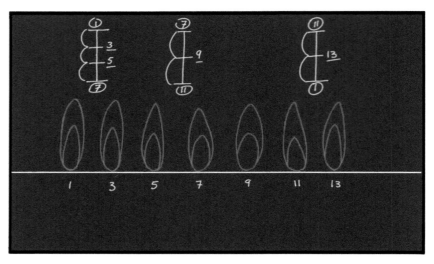

FIG 8.9 Subtle candle flame animation.

used as a glow element. On the fourth pass, I would combine A and D to get F and then finally composite E and F to get the final composite look (G) (see Figure 8.10).

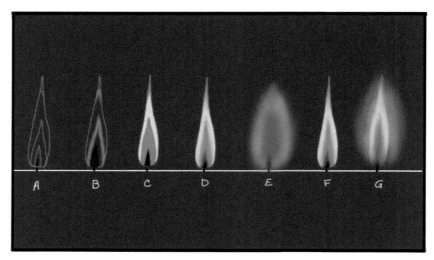

FIG 8.10 Subtle candle composite treatment.

A subtle candle animation can come in many designs. Tall, short, squat, slim, rounded, or pointy, the animation would all still have the same subtle movement. Try a variety of designs and animate them (see Figure 8.11).

Blowing out a candle flame would again involve straight-ahead animation and would take 7–14 frames. The flame would elongate and flutter in the direction the wind is blowing (see Figure 8.12).

As the flame goes out, it is immediately followed by a trail of smoke that snakes up from the wick (1) in the direction the flame flows, then dissolves off. The smoke can be dissolved off by mechanical means, in camera, or by simply animating it to make it appear thinner and thinner, eventually appearing as a thin line (11) and then nothing (15) (see Figure 8.13).

The fluttering of the flame animation could last a short or long time, depending on the direction you are given, or it may never fully extinguish but flutter back to life, back to its original form,

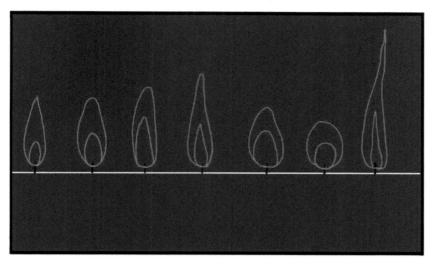

FIG 8.11 Candle flame shapes.

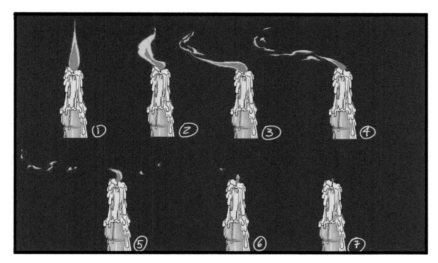

FIG 8.12 Extinguished candle flame.

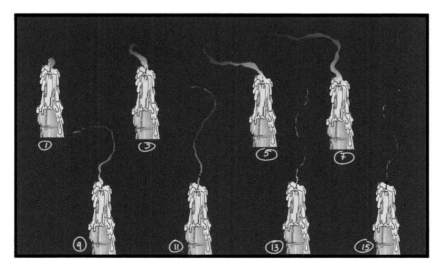

FIG 8.13 Subtle candle smoke.

and continue its subtle animation cycle. By using the illustration in Figure 8.12, for example, the animation could work in sequence from 1 through 7 but then rekindle to 1 again. Candles can emit smoke from the flame also. The smoke would emanate from the tip of the flame and snake upward, following the swaying action initiated by the animation of the candle (see Figure 8.14).

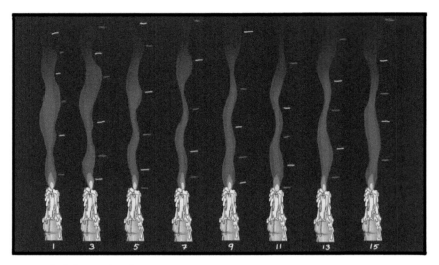

FIG 8.14 Candle flames with smoke.

Let's next go up in scale to a torch fire. Torches have been used as a light source for a long time. Usually, one end of a wooden stick is covered in pitch, tar, wax, or some sort of combustible material twisted around one end of a stick. It will burn for long periods of time to light the way as it is carried through dark caverns or dungeons or placed in a sconce on a wall to light the way in dark passages. The fire on a torch can have a variety of textures and like a candle can animate in a regular rhythmic movement but with a more robust whipping action. First let's look at a simple flame design. Igniting the torch and animating the torch being enveloped by the flame and reaching full volume will take only 17 frames for this example. It can take less or even more time—that's up to you—but I would not recommend anything faster unless the torch were doused in gasoline! (see Figure 8.15.)

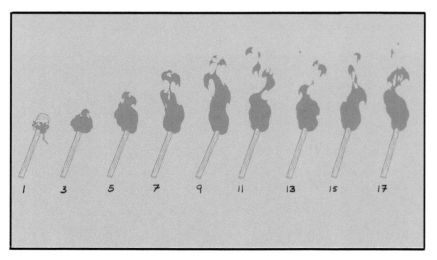

FIG 8.15 Simple torch flame.

The outside silhouette moves upward in a rippling manner. Intermittent open areas within the flame may move up with the flow of the overall silhouette of the fire expanding and breaking off in a variety of shapes and lengths that dissipate quickly as they do (one to three frames), or the flame can stretch back in the direction from which it is being carried, producing a tail. The base of the flame constantly feeds the overall body of flames (see Figure 8.16).

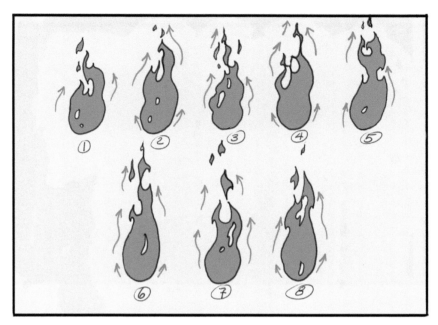

FIG 8.16 Torch silhouette animation.

The flame itself can be quite active and swirl round the torch end, twisting and snaking around the top stub. The twister-like action is very textural and obviously more complex, with more pencil millage, and is time-consuming to produce. But sometimes if the effect is prominent in a shot, it's worth the extra effort and time that it takes to produce! (see Figure 8.17.)

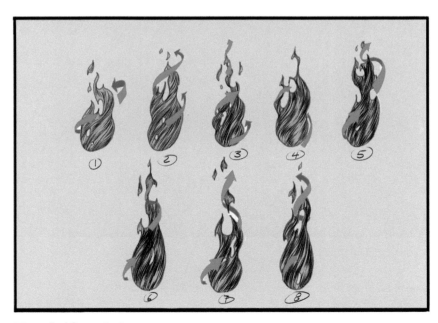

FIG 8.17 Torch flames animation.

Whether the torch is in a stationary position or is being carried around and swung back and forth will be the determining factor for the size and action of the flame. A torch that is swung about will appear to almost extinguish itself in the action, depending on the speed at which it is swung (see Figure 8.18).

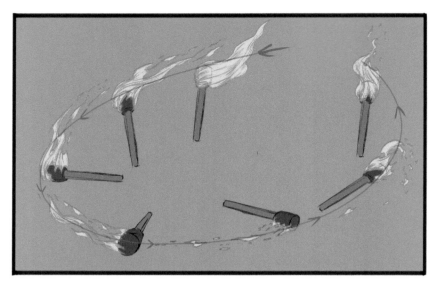

FIG 8.18 Rapid moving torch.

After the torch swung, the fire dims to small flames then blossoms again as the torch settles, allowing the flames to feed on the oxygen in the air again. The flame is in a constant state of compression and expansion as it swirls around the torch stub.

There are many designs you can try for a torch flame. Here are a few with and without textures. Try drawing as many variations as you can for practice (see Figure 8.19).

FIG 8.19 Torch flame variations.

Try some more simplistic or cartoony examples as well (see Figure 8.20).

The animation of larger-scale fires such as campfires is what I like to call "controlled chaos," due to the vigorous and dynamic action as it consumes the wood.

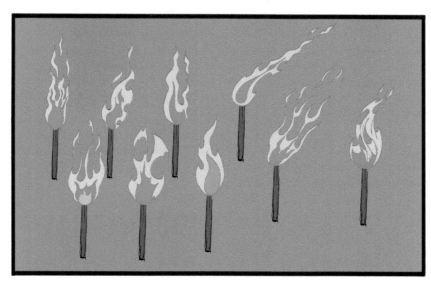

FIG 8.20 Simple torch flame design.

When animating any effect, remember to establish volume and mass. A successfully animated effect element is one that is spatially relevant and compatible with its surroundings. When animating any effect, always imagine the entire effect, not just the two-dimensional camera view. This will help you to realize the fire that is burning on the other side of the stacked wood pile, not just from the camera view angle, and will give your effect a solid three-dimensional look and feel and keep it from looking like a cardboard cutout that has no body to it. Typically, wood is stacked to allow air to feed the fire. This often results in the fire channeling upward and forming a teepee-like shape (see Figure 8.21).

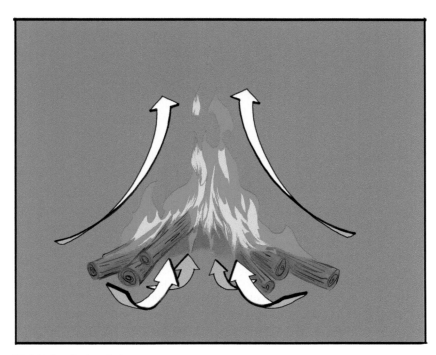

FIG 8.21 Campfire dynamics 1.

The flames run up on the slanted piles of wood, consuming the fuel. The hottest spot is usually in the center of the blaze. This is where the color separations would be concentrated, with those shapes breaking off and traveling up and blending with the rest of the flames. Keep your fire designs sharp-edged and pointy, tapering at the peak. These fires are very often lively and spirited in their animation. You can be very free and loose in your designs. Snap licks of flames off from the main body of the fire and dissipate them in two to four or six frames.

The shapes of these licks can change radically in that short time, but don't lose sight of their path of action. Otherwise you will have random shapes popping on and off haphazardly. Remember: controlled chaos! The animation should always flow smoothly upward and the silhouette should look like fire (see Figure 8.22).

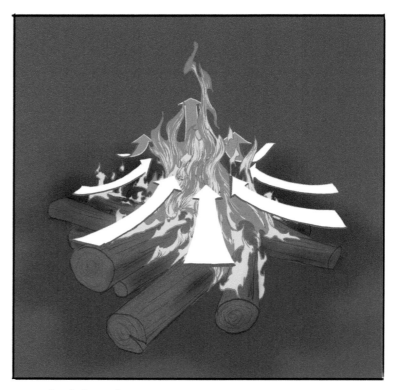

FIG 8.22 Campfire dynamics 2.

Even with a simplified design, the fire should look and feel like it's consuming the wood in all three dimensions—the front, the back, and the sides. Draw flames in the front of the fire to enhance the feeling of depth (see Figure 8.23).

Adding texture to your designs will add another positive dimension to your fire effect. Whip the flames around in a twirling pattern. Crisscross the flames in and around the stacks of wood upward to the peak of the pile. Have some of the pieces that break off twist and turn as they flare off (see Figure 8.24).

A fireplace fire is similar to a campfire, except it is supposed to direct the heat of the fire into the room in which it is located, unlike a campfire, which radiates heat all around from its core. Unfortunately, most of the heat in a fireplace rises up and out of the chimney along with the smoke it generates. The flames are fed by the air in the room and are drawn up and out the chimney flue. These forces play a part in your designs (see Figure 8.25).

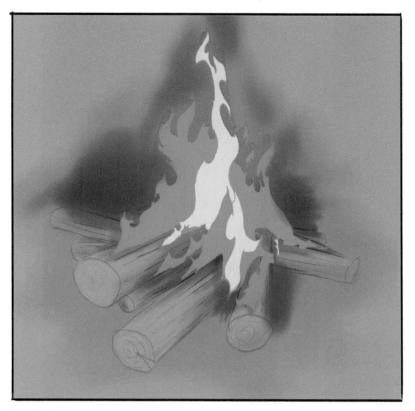

FIG 8.23 Simpler design.

FIG 8.24 Campfire with texture.

FIG 8.25 Fireplace dynamics.

The air feeds the flames as it flows under and around the logs and is drawn up the chimney (see Figure 8.26).

FIG 8.26 Airflow feeds flames.

The air will constantly be drawn up by an updraft of air that flows up the chimney, because heat rises and the open flue of the chimney allows that to happen, giving the fire a constant flow of oxygen that feeds the flames (see Figure 8.27).

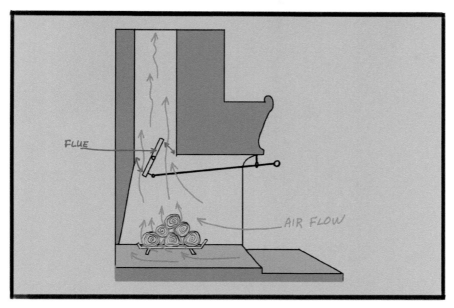

FIG 8.27 Fireplace airflow.

The chimney also affords an outlet for the smoke that is generated by the burning wood (see Figure 8.28).

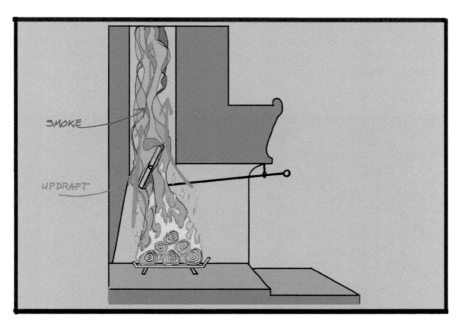

FIG 8.28 Fireplace smoke.

Sometimes a downdraft, caused by air blowing down through the chimney due to high winds outside, will almost put the fire out as it dampens the oxygen getting to the flames (see Figure 8.29).

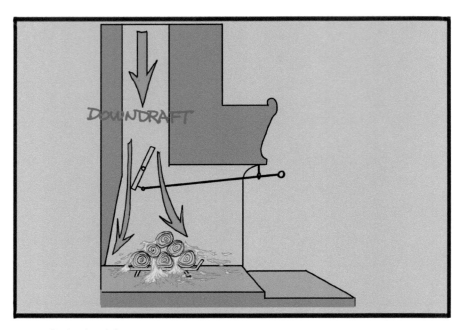

FIG 8.29 Fireplace downdrafts.

A constant burning of wooden logs in the hearth will invariably have sparks that may crackle or explode. Trapped moisture or sap trapped within the wood is heated up and boils, vaporizing into steam; as the steam expands, the wood splits and cracks open, producing snapping sounds and flying embers. Here are just a few variations of how to animate sparks, usually straight ahead and on ones! They need to be used sparingly with random timing (see Figures 8.30 and 8.31).

FIG 8.30 Fireplace sparks and embers.

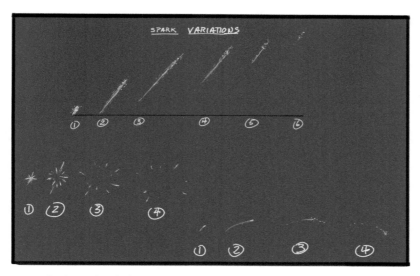

FIG 8.31 Fireplace sparks and embers.

Try some variations on fire designs or fantasy styles. Having a diverse assortment in your files or "toolbox" of designs can be of great use to you as you progress in animation. The more diversified your portfolio is, the greater your chance of finding work as an effects animator (see Figure 8.32).

FIG 8.32 Fire design variations.

A larger-scale fire, such as a forest fire, will have more texture and will usually be livelier in its animation. The flames can rise high above the ground and swirl and erupt with great explosive energy before being enveloped by the smoke the fire generates. Pieces can flare up and off in large shapes in two to eight frames (see Figures 8.33 and 8.34).

FIG 8.33 Large-scale fires.

FIG 8.34 Large flames break off.

Surges of flames shooting up to the sky and rising well above the tree lines are a common sight in forest fires. Flames that wrap around tree trunks climb up the height of the tree, consuming it rapidly, branches and leaves adding fuel to the flames (see Figures 8.35 and 8.36).

FIG 8.35 Flames wrap around trees.

FIG 8.36 Flames consuming trees.

By using multiple layers of flames, you can create an inferno. It's always wise to start by drawing a rough thumbnail of the look you wish to achieve first. A color drawing would work even better, using whatever technique you're comfortable with—whether pastels, watercolor, colored pencils, or charcoal (see Figure 8.37).

FIG 8.37 Large-scale fire thumbnail.

Once you have planned what you want your effects to look like, you need to break down the levels that it will take to accomplish the desired look. The foreground trees can have flames snaking around their trunks and at the base of the trees with detailed texture, as these flames will be the closest to camera (see Figure 8.38).

FIG 8.38 Large detailed flames.

A large mass of flames will flare on a level behind this first level behind a layer of trees. This level would require less detail but rather very large-scale flames that will tower over the trees (see Figure 8.39).

FIG 8.39 Less detailed large flames.

The third level is an overall glow that would animate very subtly. The animation of this element could be done with a single airbrushed element that can be made to look like it was pulsing and glowing by the use of the camera technique of dissolving it up and down in exposure. Fade the element off by 10% then back up to 100% in 12–18 frames. This will give the impression of intense heat. You can vary the timing of the pulse and the percentage of fading and arrive at a look that would best fit the scale of your shot (see Figure 8.40).

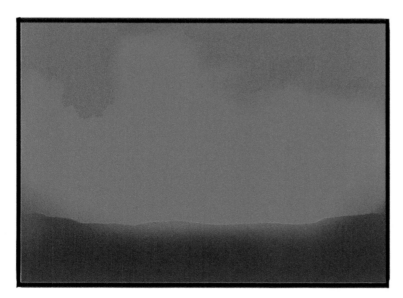

FIG 8.40 Airbrushed glow element.

The last and furthest fire effect from the camera (the bottom layer on your exposure sheet), and the most obscure, is the reuse of the level of trees and fire from the first effects level. The effective reuse of that level comes by flopping it 180 degrees parallel to the ground plane and readjusting it to fit your composition, while adding some new flames within the reused ones (see Figure 8.41).

FIG 8.41 Flop and reuse first layer of flames.

The resulting composite of all the fire elements can make for a very effective firestorm. Each level would require you setting opacity percentages for the animated fire layers to achieve the best look when you do your final composite (see Figure 8.42).

FIG 8.42 Composite of all layers.

Many times a forest fire will generate fire cyclones or vortexes of fire when conditions are right for it. Here are some illustrations that may give you some idea as to how to animate a fire cyclone or fire whirls. A fire cyclone forms when hot dry winds within a fire start to spin and pick up debris from the ground around it. These fire cyclones can last a few seconds or a few minutes, moving rapidly over the ground. The animation is like a ribbon that is wound tightly then unravels (see Figure 8.43).

FIG 8.43 Large-scale fire whirlwinds 1.

It spins upward, dragging the burning embers and ash that feed the blaze, sometimes to great heights within the forest fire, adding to the dynamics of the inferno (see Figure 8.44).

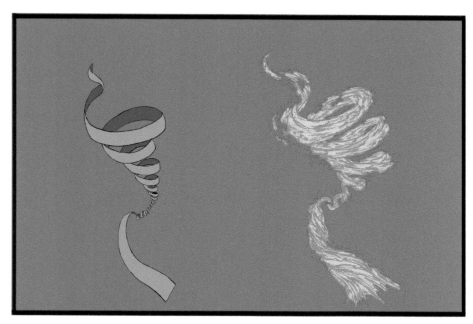

FIG 8.44 Large-scale fire whirlwinds 2.

Animate the fire cyclone by following the ribbon-like patterns winding tightly around and untwisting as it rises upward (see Figure 8.45).

FIG 8.45 Large-scale fire whirlwinds 3.

At that point, the fire cyclone can simply unravel and fragment itself, scattering flames in a circular action. Use the momentum generated from the spinning action to dissipate the flames breaking off from the main body of the fire cyclone (see Figure 8.46).

FIG 8.46 Large-scale fire whirlwinds dissipating.

CHAPTER 9

Smoke

Light-winged Smoke, Icarian bird,
Melting thy pinions in thy upward flight …

—*Henry David Thoreau*

We know that smoke is actually debris emitted from a fire. Smoke debris consists of gases, solids, and liquid particles, the substances in the fuel (wood) that do not completely incinerate in the combustion process. It can also be a forerunner to fire, such as smoldering grasses or leaves before flames burst out. Or smoke will start after a fire is established, building rapidly, and may eventually obscure the majority of the flames. Smoke is generated in fires as small as a candle flame or as large as a forest fire, but the illusion in animating the smoke is not effective if you fail to incorporate the correct scale to the corresponding fire. The volume and mass of smoke that is generated by a candle is more wispy and delicate than the volume and mass of smoke from a forest fire. The larger the fire, the greater the volume and thicker the smoke. The larger-scale smoke will be darker and obscure the surroundings, meaning that the greater the opacity, the less transparent or translucent it will be.

Distant smoke from a pile of burning leaves will appear thick and opaque. The use of color separations in your design will help to add volume (see Figure 9.1).

The color separations will define the volume of the smoke once the effect has been diffused or blurred to blend and soften the drawn smoke edges (see Figure 9.2).

Smoke that covers a wide area of a landscape can often obscure the source fire and all you see will be the smoke sweeping over the terrain. One way to effectively design such an effect is to animate an overall bottom level of smoke that establishes the mass. As this is a

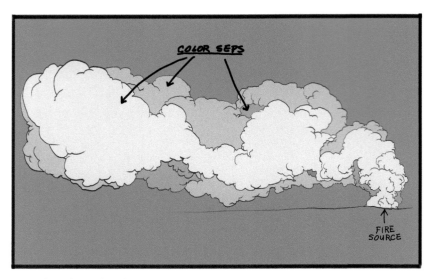

FIG 9.1 Distant large-scale smoke.

FIG 9.2 Distant large-scale smoke blurred.

base level and would be obscured by further levels of smoke on top of it, it can be very effective (see Figure 9.3).

This bottom layer of smoke can be animated as a simple cycle of eight drawings and would work fine since this is a distant and large-scale effect. When you expose the cycle on your exposure sheet, you would instruct the cameraman to blur the smoke drawings and add a light opacity. Further camera instructions would have them do eight-frame cross dissolves between all the drawings in your base smoke cycle (see Figure 9.4).

FIG 9.3 Large scale smoke.

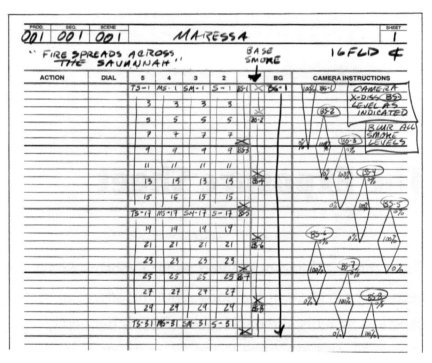

FIG 9.4 Exposure sheet with cross dissolves.

Your next order of business would be to animate one or multiple levels of smoke that would be layered one on top of another on top of the base level. I've used four separate levels to illustrate this by the use of different colors to indicate the separate smoke levels (see Figure 9.5).

FIG 9.5 Separate levels of smoke.

The separate levels of the smoke timing should work progressively more slowly from the topmost to the bottom. The top level should be slightly faster than the bottom to enhance the illusion of distance and scale (see Figure 9.6).

FIG 9.6 Top level move faster.

Expose each level with a blur and some level of opacity to achieve your final composite (see Figure 9.7).

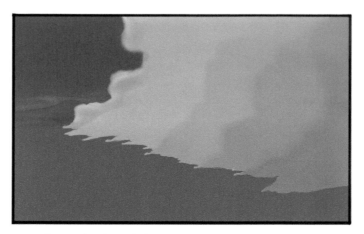

FIG 9.7 Slower smoke on bottom level.

Smoke designs can vary from a bulbous or cumulus cloud-like look to a wispy or vaporous look. It's up to you to pick and design the appropriate look for the scene. Round or bulbous shaped smoke will billow and expand, roiling as it rises and giving you the opportunity to shape the smoke by using color separations, which will add body to the overall look. The smoke animation will rise from the source, expanding and rolling inward on itself as it does. Pay close attention to the silhouette of the smoke, as this will accentuate the overall mass of the smoke and help to successfully portray the desired effect. Color separations are best used to define the shape of the smoke by using them to undercut the rolling smoke. Determine your key light source in the scene and use that as your guide to maintain a consistency in the placement of the color separations or shadowed areas of the smoke (see Figure 9.8).

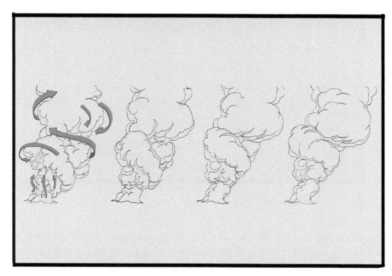

FIG 9.8 Smoke swirling action.

A more wispy or vaporous ribbon-like smoke can be animated as multiple levels that can twist and weave around themselves, with any number of opacities employed on each level, and can then be composited as one look. Animate separate levels of thin wispy smoke (see Figure 9.9). Coordinate the animation so that the individual smoke elements crisscross

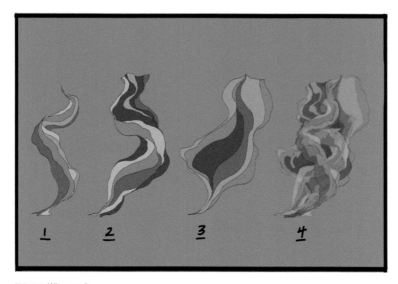

FIG 9.9 Wispy smoke.

each other in overlapping movements; when they are composited together they should flow uniformly as one mass. Image 1 plus 2 plus 3 to make up your final look of 4.

Wispy smoke works well with fire sources such as cigarettes and candles but not exclusively. It could also be used for chimney smoke. These can be animated as two or three levels that can then be composited for your final look. A simple way to start your animation of this smoke effect is to start with a single vertical line emanating from the source. The line will meander in a lazy, curvilinear fashion, arching upward (see Figure 9.10).

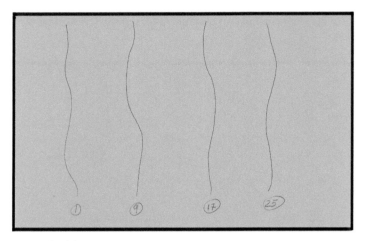

FIG 9.10 Simple line animation.

Once you animate this line, go back to your first drawn animated line and start another vertical line next to your first. The second line can crisscross the first as it animates upward (see Figure 9.11).

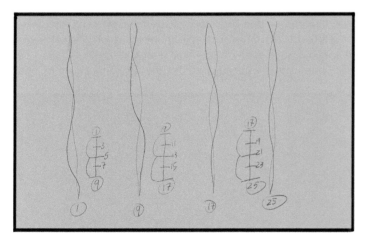

FIG 9.11 Overlapped second layer of smoke.

When you complete the animation of these two vertical lines, close them off at the top and bottom so that they can be painted (see Figure 9.12).

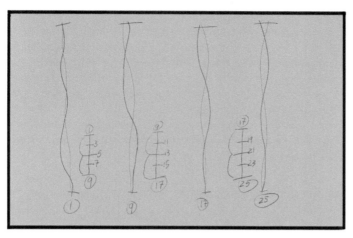

FIG 9.12 Closed of line animation.

You can then start on another level of wispy smoke that can work in unison with the first using the same technique (see Figure 9.13).

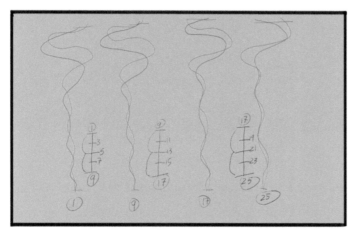

FIG 9.13 Second level of wispy smoke.

Paint the effects elements and composite the separate levels for your final smoke effect (see Figure 9.14).

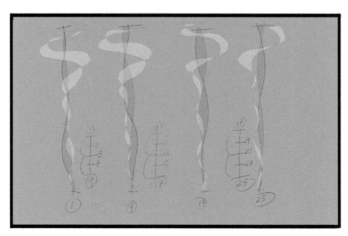

FIG 9.14 Composited smoke levels.

The look you are trying to achieve depends on how many effect levels you are willing to animate! Your relationship with your animation doesn't end with the effects once it leaves your desk. You must think ahead before you put pencil to paper. Think in terms of colored ink lines and color separations within the effect elements itself. How the effects fit into your scene is as important as actually drawing it. Visualize what opacity choices you may want for the effect! Would a blur help? What if you were to add a glow? You have a responsibility to your animation to think about all these different aspects as you're developing the effect, so that when it goes to the color models department for compositing you will have prepared the effects for all possible contingencies for the art director to work with (see Figure 9.15).

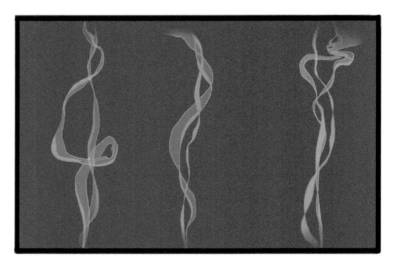

FIG 9.15 Layered small-scale smoke.

There are a great many design variations you can practice, so try many (see Figure 9.16).

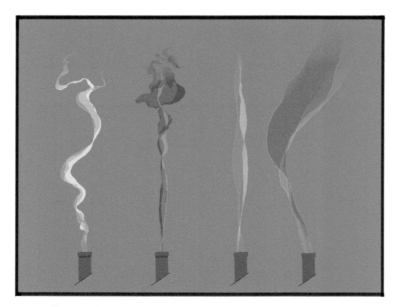

FIG 9.16 Chimney smoke variations.

Try as much variety as possible (see Figures 9.17 through 9.19).

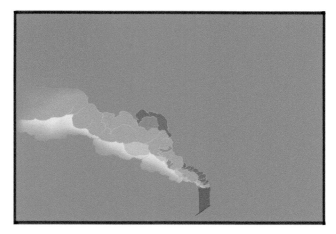

FIG 9.17 Billowy chimney smoke.

FIG 9.18 Smoke color separations 1.

FIG 9.19 Smoke color separations 2.

CHAPTER 10

Dust

What a dust we raise, said the fly upon the chariot wheel.

—Aesop

Dust is miniscule particles of earth, waste on the ground, or sand and fibers—even pollen and spores or anything that can be moved around by the air. Dust can come from sandstorms, road dust kicked up by automobiles or vehicle exhaust, and even coal mines for that matter. In other words, it's everywhere! Again, as always with any effect, be conscious of scale. Except for some variations of timing, it can move similar to smoke.

Let's start with something small, say a rock landing and skipping on the ground. The dust shoots out and away from the point of impact in a few frames (see Figure 10.1).

The initial strike by the rock on the dirt kicks up a cloud of dust and quickly grows to its maximum volume, followed by the succeeding strikes and the puffs of dust that each strike creates (see Figures 10.2 and 10.3).

FIG 10.1 Rock skipping on ground.

FIG 10.2 Dust skips up quickly.

FIG 10.3 Dust billows up.

The dust starts to settle very slowly after the rock has stopped and is no longer agitating the dirt. Set up an effects event that uses overlapping action, with the initial cloud of dust blooming to its maximum volume, followed by the rest of the rock strikes. These strikes produce blooms of dust at different stages, rising and falling back down to the ground with different timings (see Figures 10.4 and 10.5).

FIG 10.4 Skipping rock stops.

FIG 10.5 Maximum amount of dust.

A baseball player sliding into second base will kick up a cloud of dust. The momentum of the sliding player pushes the dust forward of the player and it rises rapidly through the slide. Even after the player's forward progress stops, the dust will continue to bloom forward, swirling upward and eventually slowly settling back to the ground around him (see Figure 10.6).

The downward floating action of the dust will animate more slowly than its upward action. The timing charts on the illustrations demonstrate the speed at which the dust can reach its fullest volume and eventually settle and dissipate. Note the charts between 1 and 11 as to how it will spike upward much faster than it will settle back down (19 through 61) (see Figure 10.7).

FIG 10.6 Dust builds up quickly.

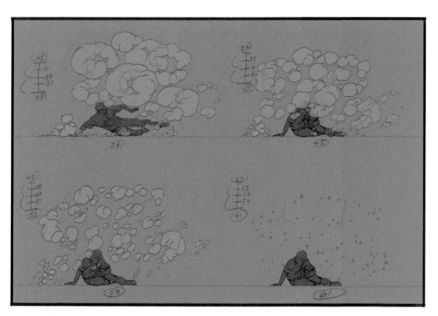

FIG 10.7 Dust settles slowly.

A rock falling directly down (1) onto a ground plane of dirt will generate a plume of dust that disperses out from the center of the contact point (3), rising and increasing in volume (3–11). The dust will rise and fall back down onto itself in a churning action (9 and 11). At this point, the volume of dust starts to develop openings in the overall appearance and breaks off in a number of separate shapes that diminish in size over time, floating downward and either settling on the ground or dissipating off entirely (17–41) before they reach the ground (see Figure 10.8).

FIG 10.8 Dust progression.

Wind sweeping across the ground will raise a plume of dust. It picks up dirt particles off the ground and coils them around in a circular "vortex" fashion, high into the air (see Figure 10.9).

FIG 10.9 Wind dust dynamics.

The design of the dust will develop "tears" in the overall configuration, following the path of action started by the overall dynamics set in motion by the wind. The plume will increase in size as the animation progresses, finally dispelling the overall volume as the tears consume it (see Figure 10.10).

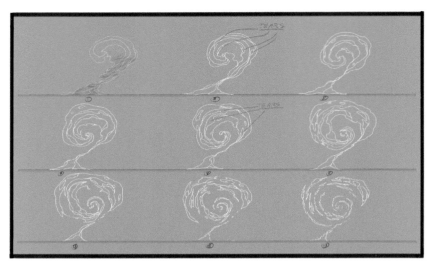

FIG **10.10** Dust vortex.

A heavier, thicker dust effect such as soot will rise only slightly above the ground plane and settle back to the ground with little or no breaking off of smaller shapes. Again, here the dust rises up quickly and then gently settles slower, moving mostly parallel to the ground plane and diminishing in volume as it does (see Figure 10.11).

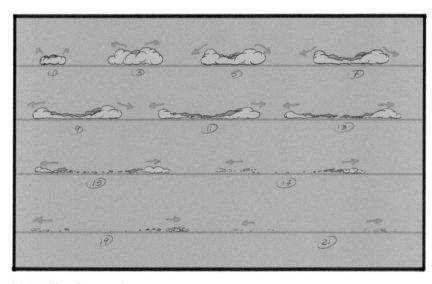

FIG **10.11** Heavy dust progression.

This type of dust effect would radiate out similarly to a ripple on water. Use an ellipse coordinating with the perspective grid in the scene (see Figure 10.12).

It would radiate out from the impact point (see Figure 10.13).

Keep in mind, however, that the actual dust animation would move in more of an asymmetrical manner, unlike the smooth and even shapes of a water ripple. Break up the silhouette so as to avoid a symmetrical design with the use of high and low points, as well as some shapes leading the main body of your animation and some trailing behind (see Figure 10.14).

Follow the design all the way through to its conclusion, with the larger shapes lasting longer than the smaller ones. Drag some shapes along longer behind the main body and don't be

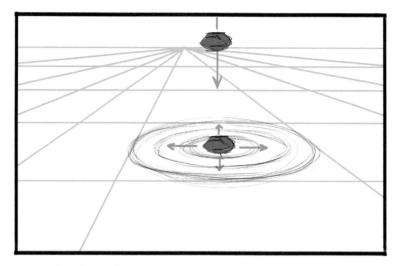

FIG 10.12 Dust radiates out from impact.

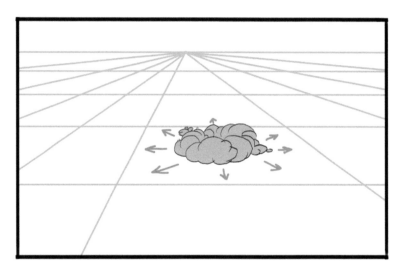

FIG 10.13 Use asymmetrical design.

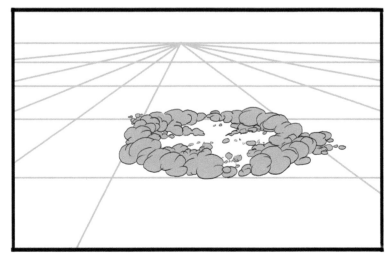

FIG 10.14 Expanding asymmetrical design.

afraid to dissipate some more quickly than others. This will make for a more interesting and natural design (see Figure 10.15).

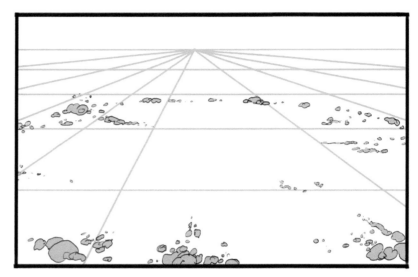

FIG **10.15** Dust dispersing.

Larger-scale dust storms would look like they moved more slowly from a distance. Most of the animated activity would take place at the base of the overall moving mass. There are very few if any shapes breaking up from the main body of the wall of dust effects. The following rough illustration will give you an idea of the dynamic forces that can be at work as a large mass of a dust storm sweeps across a landscape. Swirling aggregate at the base of the wall of dust churns violently, picking up more debris as it travels forward. The accumulated dust is elevated upward into a voluminous plume rising high above the base. This embankment of dust moves more slowly than the churning base in a more foreboding, wavelike manner, giving the impression that it will soon come crashing down on everything in its path (see Figure 10.16).

The following examples illustrate how a dust storm, through the design and timing of my rough animation, would move across a barren desert landscape. The timing charts indicate how the

FIG **10.16** Large-scale dust.

bottom and top portions would animate separately with different timing, even though it acts as one mass. I would normally animate the two levels as separate elements and treat them slightly differently at the time of the compositing stage. However, for illustration purposes I show them as one composite element with different colors to indicate the top and bottom levels.

The top portion of dust would be exposed behind the bottom portion of dust on the exposure sheet, and they would be working independently of each other (see Figure 10.17).

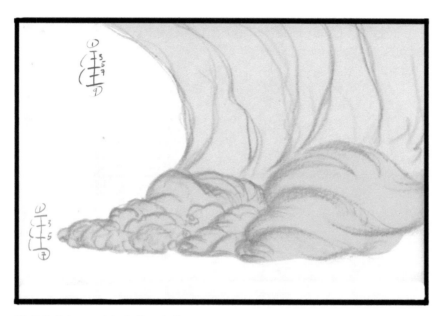

FIG 10.17 Timing separate levels of large dust 1.

The bottom portion, or the top level, of dust (red) animates on thirds timing-wise, moving a bit faster than the top portion (blue) of dust, which works behind it and has even timing, moving a bit more slowly (see Figures 10.18 through 10.20).

FIG 10.18 Timing separate levels of large dust 2.

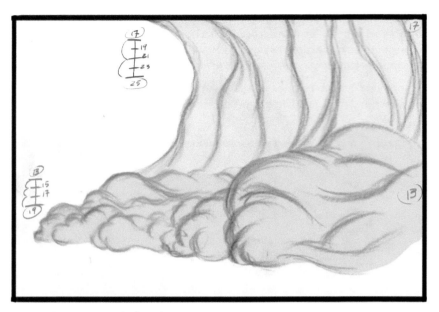

FIG 10.19 Timing separate levels of large dust 3.

FIG 10.20 Timing separate levels of large dust 4.

The final illustration here indicates that the top portion of the dust or backmost dust animation level can cycle back to animation drawing 1 from the last (33). This will save you some work because it animates behind the topmost element, that is, the bottom portion dust element. They can work independently of each other quite nicely (see Figure 10.21).

Dust whirlwinds, tornadoes, cyclones, or however you want to label them, would animate similarly to fire whirlwinds. They spin counterclockwise for those animating in the northern hemisphere and clockwise in the southern hemisphere! The designs would be a more sketchy line in nature, with a chaotic feel to the spinning action and a more sustained action as they move across the terrain. There are any number of designs you can try and I would recommend researching as many as you can find.

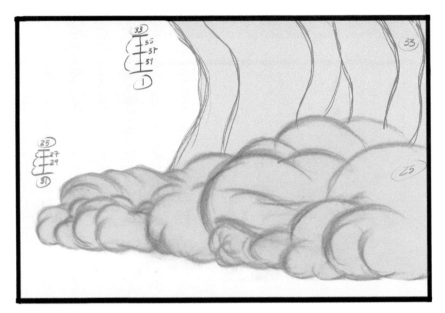

FIG 10.21 Timing separate levels of large dust 5.

Long funnel-like shapes of varying thicknesses move quickly at the base and very little at the top. Debris at the base of some would be very dense, as dirt and other loose objects are picked up and whisked about in the ensuing chaos. Each of these elements, such as dirt, fence posts, vehicles, or even parts of structures, would need to be animated as separate elements that would be combined later in the final composite. Some might be skinny on top and broad on the bottom or vice versa. Some may be broad overall. I would start out roughing out the animation to get a good feel for the overall moves, then go back and do a cleaned-up drawing of speed lines on top of those drawings to indicate the speed at which they spin, using the roughs as my guides for the overall broad movement. Here I try out some designs (see Figure 10.22).

FIG 10.22 Dust whirlwinds or tornadoes.

Next I would draw the speed lines that I would use in my final design of the effect to indicate the direction of the swirling mass and the overall look for my design (see Figure 10.23).

FIG 10.23 Tornado speed lines.

Once I have a design that I am pleased with, I animate the action in rough form, working out the staging according to the landscape and what the directions call for. Don't bother with the speed lines at this stage. You want to get the broad action first before you work on the details. This is the crucial step in your animation that will establish the scale and timing at which the tornado will animate in terms of the speed at which it travels over the land (see Figure 10.24).

FIG 10.24 Broad, large-scale tornadoes.

The broader or more massive the design, the slower the tornado will look like it's traveling overland. The longer it takes for the speed lines to travel its circumference, the more massive in scale it will look. The tornado may be several thousand feet in circumference and will take the appropriate amount of time for the speed lines to make the journey around its circumference and back again. The speed lines need to match the scale accordingly. The debris cloud at its base will help with the scale you wish to convey. Of course, this is a separate element, so be sure to match its scale to that of the tornado body. Large objects being tossed around as debris in this element can help sell the overall scale of the effect. A silo breaking up or a truck being tossed about can be very convincing, but don't worry about details in these objects; a well-drawn silhouette of the object is really all that's needed (see Figure 10.25).

FIG 10.25 Tornado with debris.

Here's a technique on how to animate speed lines for a broad-scale tornado. First, the basic roughed-out silhouette is animated (see Figure 10.26).

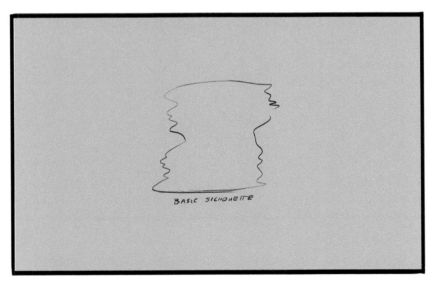

FIG 10.26 Tornado silhouette animation.

The next step is to animate dense shapes using speed lines that travel around the contours of the tornado form and animate right to left. Scatter them over the tornado silhouette to balance the design with a variety of sizes and shapes, leaving well-defined negative areas. The shapes at the top clearly delineate the perspective of the tornado as very high above the viewer's eyeline down to the ground plane, giving the tornado a sense of breadth and height (see Figure 10.27).

FIG 10.27 Broad, large-scale tornado speed lines.

Now add a layer of longer strokes that encompasses the whole silhouette and ties all the broad-stroke speed-line designs, giving it more of a sense of body and form (see Figure 10.28).

FIG 10.28 Second level of speed lines.

When all the elements are combined (the rough silhouette, the broad shapes, and the long strokes), the slight differences in timing and animation nuances that come from animating them separately from one another will enhance the chaotic feel of the overall animation. The timing difference between the levels will not be that different, but by treating the longer-stroke animation with a slightly blurrier look than the more densely shaped level, it will give the tornado a greater feeling of depth within the mass. Finally, by closing off the lines of your rough silhouette animation, filling it in with a solid color, and compositing it under your other levels with the long-stroke animation on the very top and a level of dust and debris swirling around the base of the tornado, you should get a very fine looking effect (see Figure 10.29).

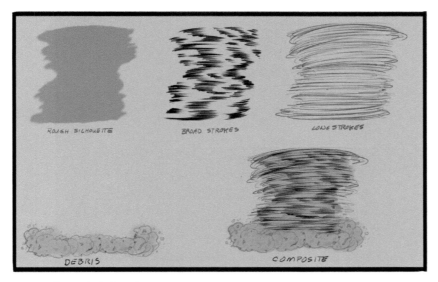

FIG 10.29 Separate levels of tornado.

You may think you're finished with the effect, but let us not forget that the clouds in the sky where the top of the tornado is joined need to have some animation also. Otherwise it would look disjointed, with the tornado animating against a static sky. Of course, a simple way is to animate the clouds in a counterclockwise direction but not necessarily at the same speed. The clouds can move more slowly than the tornado. The force of the tornado is drawing the clouds down from the center and could be animated as a separate element exposed under the very bottom level of animation (the silhouette) but on top of the background level.

First, animate a spiral poised at the top and center of the tornado that covers the expanse of the cloud formation (see Figure 10.30).

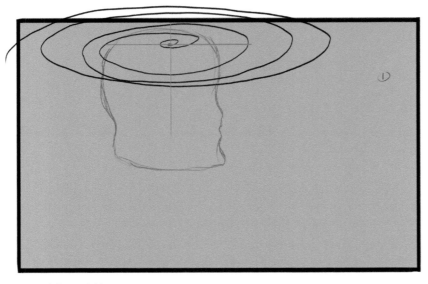

FIG 10.30 Animate spiral 1.

Once you're happy with the scale and proportions of the spiral, animate it in an expanding counterclockwise motion (see Figure 10.31).

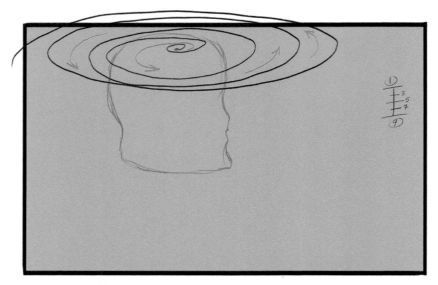

FIG 10.31 Animate spiral 2.

Use an even timing in the animation, like you see in my timing charts on the side in the illustrations (see Figure 10.32).

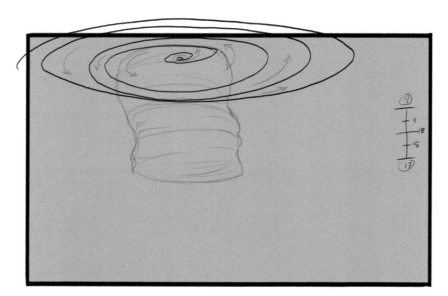

FIG 10.32 Cloud spiral expands 1.

Continue the spiral animation until you have completed the full scope of your animation. The cloud animation should work in communion with the tornado animation. Here I've animated the clouds for a total of 33 frames, my final frame (see Figure 10.33).

Now I need to return to my first spiral animation and add detail to make it look like clouds. On a separate sheet of paper, I add my cloud design, following the spiral as my guide. The cloud design will follow the spiral guide animation, so design with the idea that these clouds

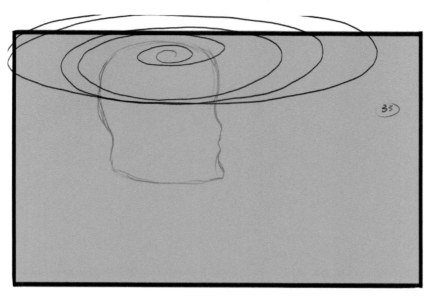

FIG 10.33 Final spiral animation.

will be animating and simplify the shapes so that they will be easy enough to follow from one key drawing to another (see Figure 10.34).

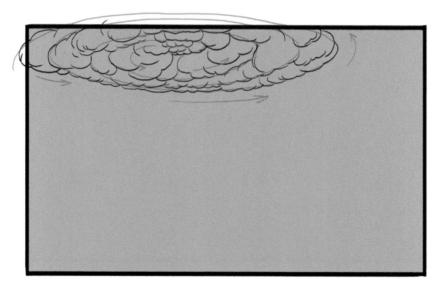

FIG 10.34 Design clouds to match spiral animation.

Here are some examples of how to animate speed lines to mimic the look of a tornado in the following illustrations. Animate broad speed-line masses, making sure that you are consistent with following those masses right to left (see Figure 10.35).

Here, I've used some colored lines to indicate the approximate shapes traveling around the cylindrical shape of this tornado. Note that they are not straight, vertical lines but are more irregular, keeping the overall look amorphous in nature rather than even. As the overall silhouette animates, the vertical lines "breathe," or expand and contract subtly, while the top and bottom maintain the cylindrical shape. The perspective must remain consistent,

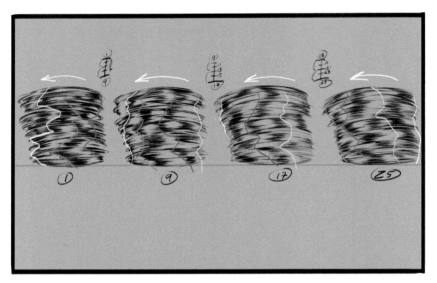

FIG **10.35** Speed line progression 1.

perpetuating our awareness of the height and mass of a gargantuan tornado effect (see Figure 10.36).

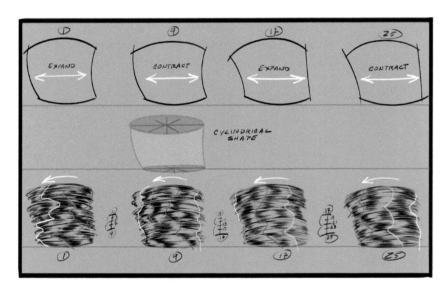

FIG **10.36** Speed line progression 2.

The thinner the design of your tornado, the faster the speed lines will spin around it. Speed lines would travel faster around a circumference of 200 feet than they would a tornado of several thousand. So be sure you match the scale correctly! Even though the design is different, the animation techniques that I've illustrated for the broader tornado would still apply to the thinner ones. Once the timing dynamics have been established, animating a cone-shaped tornado should be easier to do. The wider or broader mass at the top of the tornado would animate at a slower rate than the thinner portions at the bottom, while the middle would fluctuate somewhere in between the faster and slower rates. As the progression of rough animation drawings in Figure 10.37 indicates, the lower portion of the

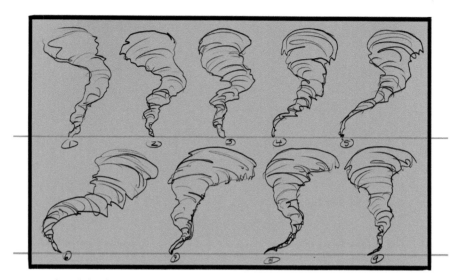

FIG 10.37 Dust whirlwinds or tornadoes.

tornado moves faster laterally than the top portion does, due to its faster gyrations. So it would seem like it would be leading the direction that the tornado was moving in.

When the speed lines go on for the finished look, I make sure that I have the bottom gyrate at least twice as fast as the top (see Figure 10.38).

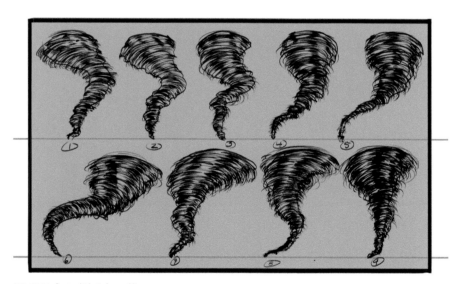

FIG 10.38 Dust whirlwind speed lines.

Once my animation is complete, I composite it using the same elements multiple times. In other words, I create two or even three layers of the same element, over each other, depending on the "look" that I have visualized in my initial thumbnails or concept drawings. Each of the layers receives a different blur or diffusion, maybe a separate brightness or contrast and even color variations (see Figure 10.39).

Wind effects animation can be represented by a series of sketchy lines or smudges. These may be thin lines produced from the point of a pencil or pen, broader lines from the side of

FIG 10.39 Dust whirlwinds concept.

a pencil, or an even broader and softer smudged look produced by a Conté crayon or hard or soft charcoal stick, which requires a lot of control (see Figure 10.40).

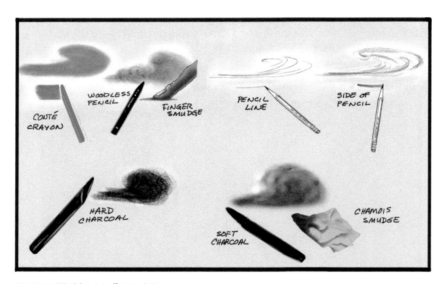

FIG 10.40 Wind drawing effects techniques.

Tones, Shadows, and Highlights

Keep your face always toward the sunshine and shadows will fall behind you!

—Walt Whitman

Late in the 1980s, *tones* came to be used copiously in animated feature films as well as television commercials that used animated characters, thus creating a great need for effects animators to handle the work load. Tones and shadows had been used in animation long before then but never so extensively or so extravagantly. Their use required that they be painted black and shot in camera at a percentage that covered the characters, would sometimes muddy their colors, and were very often distracting, so they were used sparingly and usually for dramatic effect only. The broad use of tones and shadows in animation turned out to be great news for effects animators because it meant a lot of work! Tones and shadows were applied to animated characters to effectively fit in with live-action surroundings and actors, because it gave them a more three-dimensional look, especially when used with the existing light source of the locale. They started being used in animation even more soon after, giving the animation a more polished and sophisticated look, especially with the advent of the computer in the animation ink and paint process. Adding tones to a character became a simpler and more efficient process then, blending in with the character's color palette and avoiding the muddy blend from before. Now the composites could use the tone mattes to darken the values of existing colors rather than just laying black on top of the colors.

While tones may look simple to do, they're not! They require careful planning in their design on the part of the effects animator to avoid crawling lines and unwanted fluctuations of the effect over the character, especially the face. Tones are simple mattes that isolate areas on a character that you want to treat in a certain way. You may wish to put areas out of focus, diffuse, blur, or brighten them, or as with tones darken specific areas to indicate the direction of a light source, or all of the above. By using the key drawings of the character animation, you anchor the tones properly to the character's movements and gyrations and then follow the same procedures of breakdowns and inbetween work by assistant effects animators, who follow up the animator to complete the traditional animation process.

Figure 11.1 shows you the setup as it applies to the procedure for animating tones on a character. The character animation drawing is first placed on the animation disc, then a clean sheet of animation paper is placed on top of that so that the tone matte works one to one with the character animation at all times.

FIG 11.1 Tone animating setup.

Once the first key drawing is done, the next character key drawing is placed on the disc and another blank animation sheet is placed on that in order to make the corresponding tone drawing key. This process is repeated until all the key drawings in the scene are done. You can have as many as five key drawings that you can "flip" on your animation disc at one time. You are flipping the character drawing and the tone drawing at the same time so that you are certain the tones and the character are working together properly (see Figure 11.2).

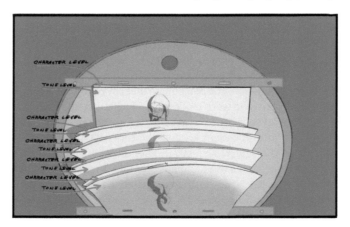

FIG 11.2 Match tone extremes with character extremes.

The design of the tones needs to follow the contours of the character, be they the chiseled contours of the hero, the dowdy features of a sidekick, or a complex zombie character. They must be solidly arranged on that character so that they animate one to one with the characters as they move around; they must easily be followed up by the assistants when the scene comes to them for completion. The tones are designed to follow the high and low contours on the character's face and body, as well as the costume or clothes he or she is wearing. The following illustrations (Figures 11.3 through 11.8) show a variety of ways

I have designed the tones on a detailed character. Whenever you have a large or long area, such as the thighs or arms, try to avoid following all the nooks and crannies. Instead, try to keep a nice smooth curving line that follows the contours of the body part. When I draw out the tone outside the silhouette of the character I "slop" the line around him.

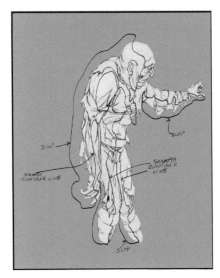

FIG 11.3 Tone line work.

FIG 11.4 Tone filled in.

FIG 11.5 Tone trimmed by character.

FIG 11.6 Final look of tone.

The reason for this is that when the tone is painted black and composited onto the character, the character will trim the tone matte to itself, illuminating the slop line and basically cutting the tone to its own silhouette. I have given the tone an opacity in this illustration to show you the parts of the tone, the "slop," that will be cut.

Figure 11.5 shows you how the tone will look in composite without the slop. The reason for the slop line is simple: it's faster to draw than following the character's silhouette and, often when compositing the line that you trace around, the silhouette can shrink back inside the silhouette! Don't ask me why, but sometimes it just does. So it's better to be safe than sorry and slop it out whenever you need to.

139

Here's another possible version of the tone on the same character but with simpler line work that can be just as effective.

Tones can also be used to create rim lights around a character to create a backlight effect. This is a more complex method and harder to control and maintain without the tone sliding around.

FIG 11.7 Tone for rim.

FIG 11.8 Rim lite tone.

A more effective way to animate a highlight is by drawing a tone around the character's silhouette just inside it and slopping the junk out away from the character. With a few strategically placed highlights in areas that stand out here and there, this is an easier and more controllable method of doing rims.

By using this method, the color modeler would then be able to use the same method in illuminating the slop and instead of darkening the color values would instead brighten them where the rim was and blur that area to get the same desired effect of a rim light, as in Figure 11.7.

Here's an example of doing a bottom light effect on a menacing character. You can do it as a straight tone matte with an opacity effect (A) or use that same tone matte, blur it, and add a slight opacity to get a more subtle gradated look (B) (see Figure 11.9).

FIG 11.9 Bottom light effect with tone.

The intensity of the light source will determine the overall tone on the character. The more extreme the light source, such as a spotlight (A), the more light it casts onto the subject and the less of a tone on the subject. The weaker or duller the light source, such as a light bulb or a candle (B), the less light that will be cast onto the subject and the greater the tone on the subject. More light equals less tone. Less light equals more tone. Of course, all this is predicated by what the director and art director feel is the appropriate mood for the shot (see Figure 11.10).

FIG 11.10 Different light sources.

The following deals with terminology: One character in a room with one key light source. It's important to keep in mind the position of the light source so that the tone corresponds to the angle of incidence at which the light source strikes the character (red hash marks) (see Figure 11.11).

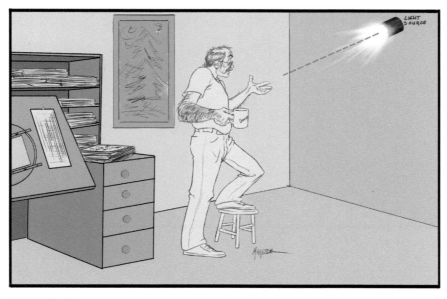

FIG 11.11 Key light source.

For these illustrations, I first lower the opacity of the character so that the line work of the effect is more clearly defined. We'll start with a simple *tone* (see Figure 11.12).

FIG **11.12** Simple tone line.

Now I fill in the art and give it the proper opacity; I expose it over the character (see Figure 11.13).

FIG **11.13** Tone filled in.

The next term is *tone for rim light*. This is a tough one to control and I would use it sparingly! (see Figure 11.14).

FIG 11.14 Tone for rim line work.

Now we can see the *tone for rim light* with the art filled in and proper exposure (see Figure 11.15).

FIG 11.15 Tone for rim look.

Next, let's do a straight *cast tone*. The cast tone is a shadow that has been cast onto the character from an object or when a character walks into a shadowy area such as between two buildings in a setting. I've illustrated the angle that the light travels to the subject with red hash marks so that the tone for the shadow is cast onto the character at the proper angle. This is a good way to keep track of the tone on a character so that it always lays correctly on him or her, whether the object casting the shadow is moving or the character is moving and the object is stationary. Either way, the light source in this case is in a constant position (see Figure 11.16).

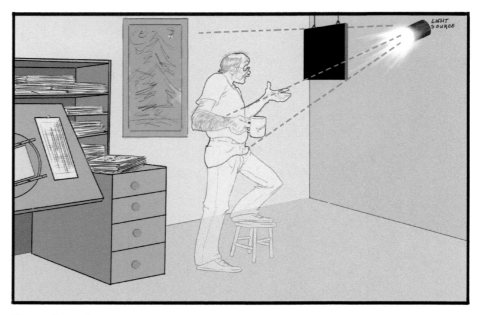

FIG 11.16 Cast tone line up.

Note: When animating a tone over a character's face, draw around the eye to keep it clear. *The eyes of a character are extremely important to the character's personality, so let the art director make the color adjustments to the eyes rather than muddying them with a tone.* Here's the cast tone filled in and with opacity (see Figure 11.17).

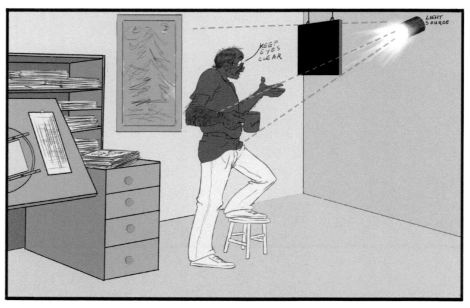

FIG 11.17 Cast tone.

Here's what happens when the object casting the shadow moves, along with where the tone is cast onto the character according to the angle of the light source (see Figure 11.18).

FIG 11.18 Cast tone moving over character.

Now let's animate a *rim light*. This is an easier and more efficient method that I mentioned earlier in the chapter. It is easier in that it's easier to control, thereby making it more efficient to animate. We'll concentrate on the edges of the character's silhouette and the high points that may catch a glint of light, which may help to accent and give the overall form a sense of roundness (see Figure 11.19).

FIG 11.19 Rimlite.

The rim light will look something like this once it is painted for composite (see Figure 11.20).

FIG 11.20 Painted rimlite.

After the proper treatment in color models, with blur and the addition of brightness and color, this is the final effect (see Figure 11.21).

FIG 11.21 Rimlite final look.

Next, let's animate a *cast shadow*, from the same light source and from the character onto his surroundings. This would indeed be called a *shadow*; since it is being cast from the character and at a more oblique angle due to the angle of light, it would be a *cast shadow*. The shadow, along with the proper tone matte, will make a convincing lighting effect (see Figure 11.22).

FIG 11.22 Cast shadow and tone.

A *drop shadow* or *puddle shadow* is simply a circular or elliptical shape under the character when a simple shadow effect is called for. No defining character shape, just a shape to anchor the character to the ground. Here, we have an overhead light source (see Figure 11.23).

FIG 11.23 Drop shadow.

A traveling light source can affect the volume or thickness of the tone (see Figure 11.24).

Another type of highlight is adhered to the character within the silhouette, representing a shine or a glossy surface. These types of glints or highlights must be consistent in their

FIG **11.24** Heavy to light tone animation.

thickness and shape and overall volumes. Keeping these highlights at a consistent distance from the edge of the silhouette and following the contours of the surface is a must! You don't want the highlight "floating" over the body or the object on which you place it, unless the light source moves (see Figure 11.25).

FIG **11.25** Highlite.

On occasion you may come upon a scene that calls for not only a key light source but a secondary light source as well. In this type of scenario, the key light will be your broad tone element, whereas the secondary can be dealt with as a highlight element. First we discuss the key light tone element (see Figure 11.26).

FIG 11.26 Key light source.

The secondary tone element can be applied using a highlight tone such as is illustrated here (see Figure 11.27).

FIG 11.27 Secondary light source.

When these two tone elements are combined, the key light tone as a tone element and the secondary light tone element as a highlight element, giving each a blur for soft edges, you get the following look. Neither has a sharp edge and neither dominates the other. But the effect that is achieved is one that gives the character a three-dimensional look (see Figure 11.28).

FIG 11.28 Combination of light sources.

CHAPTER 12

Rocks, Props, and Things

Water continually dropping will wear hard rocks hollow.

—*Plutarch*

When animating rocks, there are times when all that is required would be a simple traceback, such as when the rock animates through a scenario in only a few frames. Here, all you need do is to trace the rock back for each succeeding frame and use it for those few frames without any change in its perspective. Note that this would be animated on ones (meaning that every frame in the shot is drawn); the rock would travel the distance of its own diameter for each frame (see Figure 12.1).

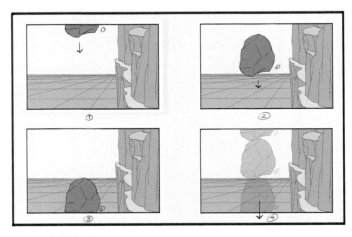

FIG 12.1 Rock falling fast on ones.

This is the simplest setup that you may run across. The rock is large and there are no rocks following the large one as it falls through the frame. It's simple and straightforward and does the job adequately for this particular setting. When I animate a rock falling in a shot, I like to add smaller ones that fall with it, overlapping the action of the larger one. This makes for a more visually interesting composition. I find that it's always best to tumble them a bit as they are falling, rather than just tracing the same shapes and textures over and over again as I animate, drawing the rock in its full three dimensions (see Figure 12.2).

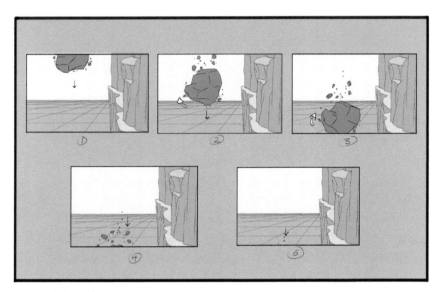

FIG 12.2 Rocks tumbling.

Large and small rocks can best be animated as simple geometric shapes on your first rough pass. No need to bother with details on this pass. The layout will have the rock effect elements drawn to the proper scale and shapes from the layout artist. There is usually a certain amount of latitude for the effects animator to alter the designs. So study the designs to determine if they merit any changes (see Figure 12.3).

FIG 12.3 Layout.

At this time, you need to convert the rock designs to simple graphic shapes in order to animate them in place of the detailed rock elements in the layout. You will be able to animate those shapes with greater ease by tumbling those simple shapes and be able to establish your timing much more quickly than if you had to worry about the details of each individual rock as you animate (see Figure 12.4).

FIG 12.4 Animate simple shapes.

When animating rocks, whether it's a single rock or boulder or a group of rocks, remember to keep it interesting. What do I mean by that? Treat the group of rocks you're animating as one unit, by animating the group of rocks falling by the diameter of the unit itself to establish your timing (see Figure 12.5).

FIG 12.5 Groups of rocks as a unit.

Treat the larger rocks individually within the group as they fall by tumbling them. Don't overdo it, however! A slight pitch and yaw as they fall is all that is required; although it may not be seen, it will give a more natural feel overall to the animation of the group of rocks (see Figure 12.6).

FIG **12.6** Twist and tumble large rocks.

On another pass or as a separate level altogether, you may want to animate ancillary groups of smaller rocks trailing behind the larger group—but mix it up, by having some medium-sized and different-shaped ones as well. This will give the impression of debris that has shifted and has been displaced as the larger ones have fallen and dragged them along. It will make it a bit more visually interesting (see Figure 12.7).

FIG **12.7** Smaller rocks trial behind.

Finally, after all the rough animation has proven successful and your timing is approved, you can clean up your animation using the graphic stand in shapes to make new cleaned-up drawings, on a separate sheet of animation paper (see Figure 12.8).

It's safe to assume that when an object animates across the screen, up or down or side to side, it will move the distance of its own diameter. You can animate on ones or twos or 24 frames or drawings per second of film. When animating on ones, you will draw every frame. If you animate on twos, you would only draw 12 drawings or half the frames per second of film, exposing each drawing for two frames.

FIG 12.8 Cleaned up and finished animation.

Those images will move at twice their diameter when animated and may require speed lines to overlap in the space that would have been occupied by the previous drawing (see Figure 12.9).

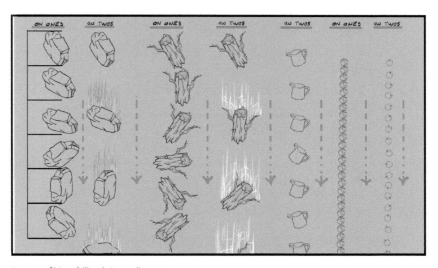

FIG 12.9 Objects falling their own diameter.

You will be passing along an exposure sheet (X-sheet) to the camera department in addition to your animation drawings when you've finished animating your shot (see Figure 12.10). The X-sheet is a great resource in helping you figure out the timing as you animate and how it will be shot on film by the camera operator. Here's how it can help you figure out your timing and what animating on ones and twos visually translates to on an X-sheet. One second of film is equal to 24 frames, and an X-sheet defines it as 24 separate frame placeholders for your animation drawings. One second on the X-sheet is also defined by three groups of eight frame divisions, so as you animate, mentally count out "thou," "sand," "one," while you visualize the effects elements animating on that blank paper in front of you. Each of these eight frame divisions translates to one syllable of the "thousand one" and are there so that you can visually break down your timing. This takes a lot of practice, but it is made easier by your use of the X-sheet (see Chapter 22).

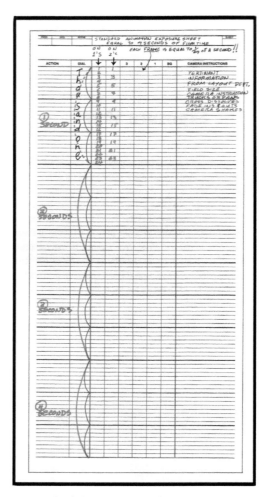

FIG 12.10 Standard animation exposure sheet.

Depending on the object or element you're animating, if it moves very quickly, you may need to add speed lines to overlap the action by filling in the dead space between the frames. This usually occurs when you are animating on ones, like the examples in Figures 12.11 through 12.13.

FIG 12.11 Use of speed lines.

FIG 12.12 Speed lines 1.

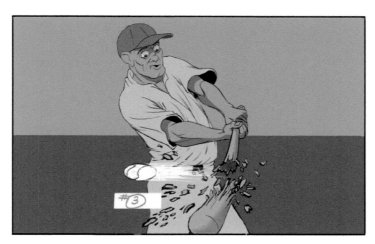

FIG 12.13 Speed lines 2.

And of course, the frame after this drawing, the ball would be out of frame or perhaps there would be some feathering of speed lines at the edge of the frame. Try without first on your pencil test to determine whether it would be necessary, and if there is too much of a pop, then add some speed lines (see Figure 12.14).

FIG 12.14 Speed lines 3.

A baseball that has been thrown by a baseball pitcher would need to be animated with speed lines and on ones. If an object such as a baseball has a number of colors, it would be best to include some of the colors in the speed lines. Another tip is to animate the object (baseball) separately from the speed lines. In this case, while the overall color of the baseball is white, the speed lines should be overall mostly white. However, since the ball has red stitching and decals on it, I would highlight the speed lines with a hint of red as well. From the batter's point of view, animate only two to three frames along with speed lines (see Figure 12.15).

FIG 12.15 Multicolor speed lines.

Normally, I would draw the speed lines on an object the length of one to one and one-half its diameter (see Figure 12.9).

With a ball being thrown at great velocity, such as a pitcher throwing a baseball, I would give it longer speed lines. Getting the ball to the catcher would only take two to three frames/drawings, but depending on the angle of the composition it could be a bit longer. In Figure 12.15, the ball would get to the catcher more quickly than in Figure 12.16. At this angle, I would probably animate the ball in three to four frames with the added speed lines.

FIG 12.16 Speed lines in perspective.

A batter swinging a bat may require multiple images of the bat and hands as he swings at the baseball. For this, I would simply recommend that you draw the speed lines as a sequence of afterimages that follow the arc that the bat describes in the action as the batter swings it (red line). Then break up the images of the bat to be used in the effect as incomplete silhouettes of the bat (1). Now, add in short strokes on a few of the more defined bat shapes while overlapping some of the subsequent speed lines of the bat images behind them (2). Fill in the rest of the speed line effect with long, sweeping lines that define the swing further (3) to complete the effect (see Figure 12.17).

FIG 12.17 Multiple image speed lines.

Bullets fired from a weapon would simply be very quick streaks. The initial frame in which the gun is being fired would show the flash and gasses (smoke) that expand as the powder is discharged, preceding the bullet from the barrel! (see Figure 12.18).

FIG 12.18 Gun smoke.

The flash would last only one or two frames as the smoke expands rapidly and as the bullet explodes from the barrel of the gun and streaks off following its trajectory, straight and true! In Figure 12.19, the bullet would only be seen as a streak of one frame, given the proximity of the gun in the composition.

FIG 12.19 Smoke and streaking bullet.

On a long shot (no pun intended), the bullet would be represented by a series of long streaks describing its trajectory in the composition as it ricochets from one surface to another (see Figure 12.20).

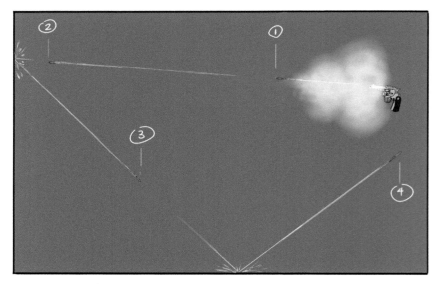

FIG 12.20 Ricocheting bullet.

Depending on the gun, you could vary the effect with the amount of smoke and even particles shooting out from the barrel. Use streaks for the particulate matter (leftover residue in the gun barrel) that may erupt from the barrel to add a nice little touch to the overall look of the effect. The streaks fly off from the barrel mouth, preceding the musket ball, and from the flintlock for a nice contrast to the smoke (see Figure 12.21).

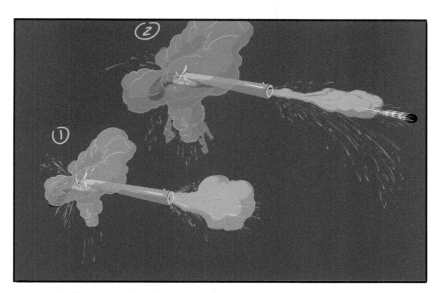

FIG 12.21 Speed lines, more smoke, and particulate streaks.

Another use of speed lines is as streaks or sparks. In Figure 12.22, I use them as sparks, as the flint causes a spark to ignite the powder of the musket flintlock device. First, I animate the sparks as the flint scrapes against the frizzen device and ignites the powder in the small pan, which subsequently ignites the powder in the musket barrel and launches the projectile (see Figure 12.22).

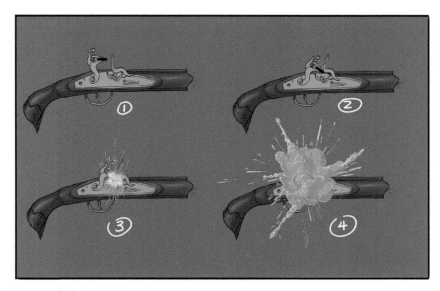

FIG 12.22 Sparks and streaks.

Another use of streaks would be for fireworks. I would combine three effects elements for the fiery tail. The first two would be streams of flames in two separate colors. You can use the same element twice by simply animating a three-to-four-frame fiery effect cycle (A) and then copying it and offsetting the timing (B) of the two by a few frames as a separate level. The third would be a three-to-four-frame animated cycle of sparks (C) that would be composited over the other two. By combining the three as one (D) effects element, you will have created a very convincing rocket tail trailing behind the rocket as it travels upward, delivering its payload high in the sky (see Figure 12.23).

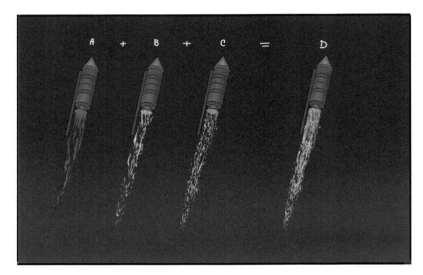

FIG 12.23 Sparks and streaks as fireworks.

Now that you have the rocket and its fiery tail animated, you would need to set up a trajectory for the rocket to travel. Draw an arc across the path you want the rocket to take and mark out the timing, or simply write the number of frames that you want the animation to last before your other effects (the fireworks explosion) takes over. Note where in the sky you want it to finally explode. By using the rocket element and the fiery tail effects cycle animation as a single effect unit element, you can move it mechanically over the path of your arc to its final destination by writing in the camera instruction column on your X-sheet how you want the scene planning department to plot the elements for the final shoot. In that column you would also write a note to scene planning: "Note, scene planning: Please call me at extension 0000 to go over these instructions." You would then, more than likely, get a call from the person who will be working on your scene. You would then probably go and sit down beside this person at his or her computer station to help make all the effects elements work in the manner you envisioned it. In today's world of computers, the scene planning department would work out the mechanics, combine all the scanned elements (character and effects) to the proper scale, and plot the move along with any other camera moves that may have been set up by the layout department (see Figure 12.24).

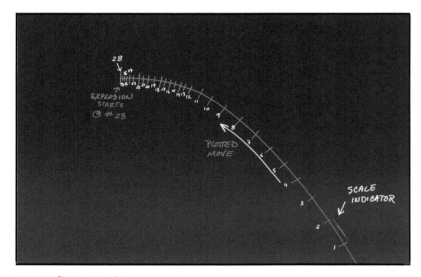

FIG 12.24 Plotting timing chart.

Next you see the rocket flying in the night sky on the path you worked out (see Figures 12.25 and 12.26).

FIG **12.25** Rocket spacing.

FIG **12.26** Exploding firework.

Fireworks are streaks of different colors animated in a series of expanding masses from one frame to the next. As the streaks expand, the ones at the top will reach an apex and slow down and diminish in intensity by making them smaller with each succeeding frame. Meanwhile, the ones on the sides and on the bottom continually expand and arc toward the ground as they diminish in size and intensity until they flicker out completely. Don't forget that this is an explosion of particles moving from the center outward in all directions, so be sure to indicate particles expanding toward camera as well as away from camera. This can be accomplished by having some of those particles growing in size before flickering out (see Figures 12.27 through 12.32).

FIG 12.27 Explosion expands.

FIG 12.28 Streaks breaking up.

FIG 12.29 Streaks turn into particles.

FIG 12.30 Sparks enhance the effect.

FIG 12.31 Sparkles outnumber the particles.

FIG 12.32 Sparkles flicker off.

Now everything is worked out, and the rocket flies through the night sky along the path you have described and worked out with your friends in scene planning. The fireworks effects animation explosion pops on at the precise spot you indicated just as the rocket and its fiery tail effects animation pops off. You and scene planning have worked hand in hand in a most collaborative way, everything works as it should, and everyone has done their job correctly. All is right with the world, and you can move on to your next shot!

Here are some simple firework designs that you can try some animation on. It gets tedious due to all the little details, but be patient—it's worth the training and discipline you will acquire as you're doing it (see Figure 12.33).

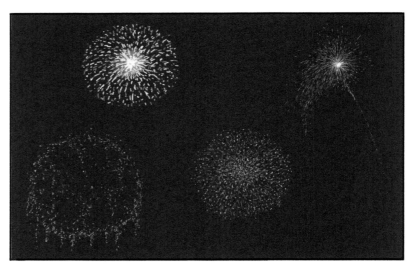

FIG 12.33 Fireworks designs.

Fireworks are designed to form certain shapes and sometimes multiple explosions within other explosions, one after another, so plan your effect carefully. Make sure you understand what your timing will be and what you want it to look like. *Plan your work and work your plan!* Here are some simplified illustrations in which I have outlined some things to think about as you plan your effect that may help you animate these large-scale firework explosions (see Figures 12.34 and 12.35).

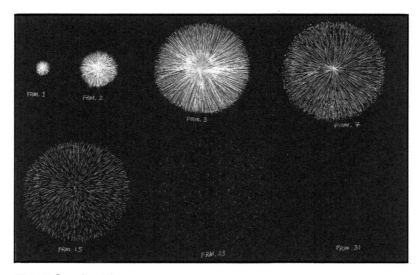

FIG 12.34 Fireworks variation.

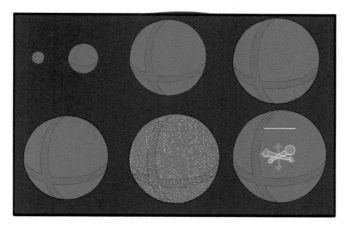

FIG 12.35 Approach a fireworks explosion as if it were an ever expanding sphere radiating out from center.

Here is the same explosion in its most basic form, a sphere (see Figure 12.36).

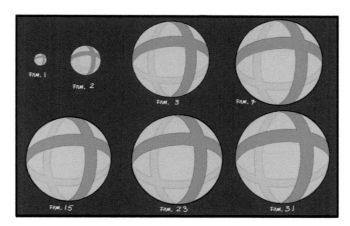

FIG 12.36 Expanding sphere in all directions.

The explosion is very fast and starts out very dense, with all the particles clumped tightly together (Frames 1 and 2). This cluster of particles will expand almost immediately to its maximum breadth, within a few frames from the initial explosion (Frame 3) (see Figure 12.37).

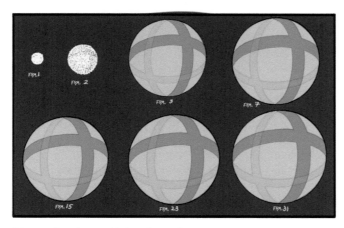

FIG 12.37 Dense in center thinning as it expands.

Try to differentiate the back plane of the explosion as well as the foremost plane as much as you can (Frame 3). The backmost plane will have the smaller particles. The foremost will be a concentration of larger particles. When the back and front planes are considered as separate and distinct planes you animate, the end result will be an explosion that is expanding in all directions, rather just a flat two-dimensional drawing (see Figure 12.38).

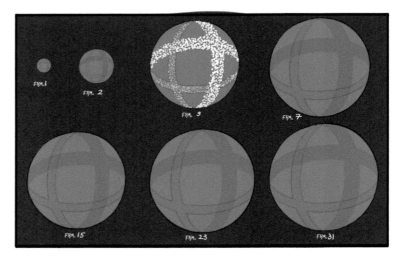

FIG 12.38 Heavier thicker particles in front.

In the back plane of the effect, the particles are smaller (Frame 7), just as the front-plane particles are bigger (Frame 15) (see Figure 12.39).

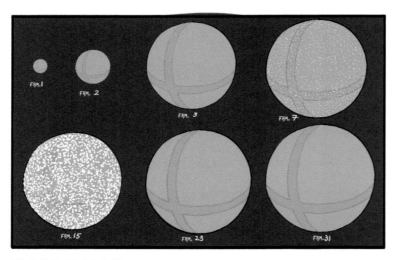

FIG 12.39 Particles in back thinner.

By distinguishing the plane in this manner, you are sure to produce a successful effect that assures your effect looks and feels like an expanding fireworks explosion (Frames 23–31). Maintaining and resolving the effect is the bulk of the work, due to the amount of "pencil millage" that goes into the animation. In these illustrations you can see that the explosion radiates outward from the center, reaches its pinnacle, then resolves over a longer period of time as the frame count below them illustrates the time it might take. This requires concentration and patience but is worth the effort (see Figure 12.40).

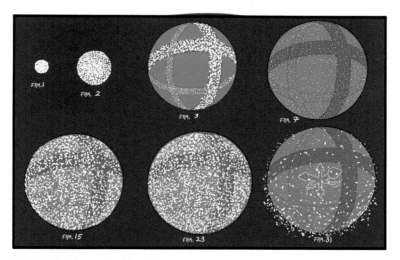

FIG 12.40 Particles expand and taper off.

Now let's talk about some of the props that you might have to deal with and how to best handle them. You'll need some of these tools to help you with drawing and animating props, simple tools that you most likely have laying around your studio—a straight-edge ruler, a circle and ellipse template, some French curve templates, a flexible French curve, and a compass. The variety you get is up to you, but I've found these to be sufficient for my needs (see Figure 12.41).

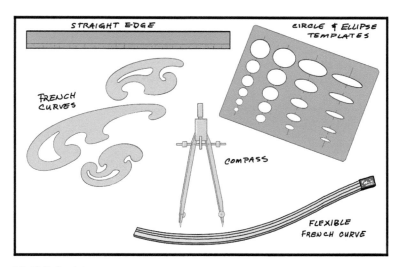

FIG 12.41 Templates.

Let's start with the hand gun or pistol I used earlier in this chapter and break it down to a simpler shape to animate. I have included as inserts the tools I used to finish the props after my preliminary freehand pass. These simple, rough handgun elements would ideally be done after the character animator did his rough animation but before they got passed on to the cleanup department. An effects animator would rough-animate the handgun, matching the rough character animation (1). They would serve as placeholders for cleanup assistants to register the character's hand around it as they finished the final character cleanup drawings. After cleanup was done, these rough gun elements would return to the effects department, along with the cleaned-up character animation, and would be used to make the final cleaned-up prop elements along with any adjustments that might be needed for proper registration (2). These guns would be done using simple geometric forms, using rectangular box shapes or tubes to form the handle and barrel (see Figure 12.42).

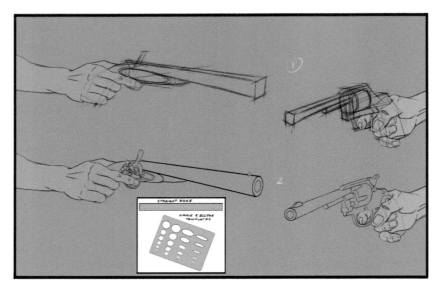

FIG 12.42 Use simple forms.

Animating props doesn't have to be difficult! If you approach this task by starting them out as simple geometric shapes, it will be a lot easier than trying to animate them in their full, final model form. So, here are some props we might find ourselves having to animate and how I would break them down. At first I would rough it out freehand. Never take anything for granted! A simple cup or pot can frustrate you if your ellipses don't match your perspective. So start by defining the correct perspective and matching your ellipses as close as possible freehand. Then use your templates to finish your drawings (see Figure 12.43).

FIG 12.43 Simple shapes.

Drawing a small rowboat or dory starts with a simple figure eight for the gunwale or the top of the sides of the boat. The boat can be as streamlined as you want, so how you draw your figure eight will determine that. From here, draw out the sides and a center line for the keel of the boat from bow to stern. Add further dimension to the keel and then rowlocks for the oars and a stern seat, frame ribbing, and as a final touch the planking lines on the hull of the boat (see Figure 12.44).

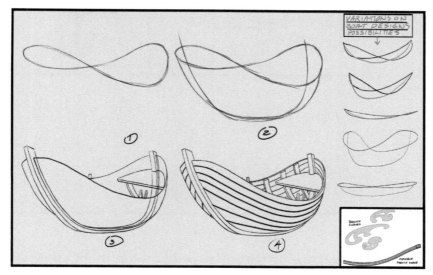

FIG 12.44 Constructing a boat.

A simple sailboat would only require the use of a straight edge and a flexible French curve after you've roughed out your boat. The flexible French curve will help with the sails as the wind fills them (see Figure 12.45).

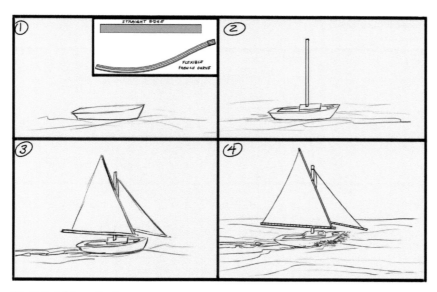

FIG 12.45 Building a sailboat.

The more complex the prop, the more time and possibly the more tools required to draw the element. The more you draw, the easier it will be for you to draw more freehand with less reliance on your tools. The tools will be there when you need them. But don't underestimate their usefulness and discard them! Using these tools to help you draw props could be the difference between a fishing boat looking solid bobbing on the water or a wooden boat looking like a rubber raft because your pencil lines are oscillating too much (see Figure 12.46).

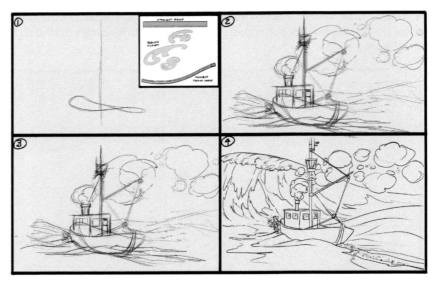

FIG 12.46 Combine tools and freehand.

A prop that is part of the layout being used as an overlay, or underlay, where characters may need to walk behind and in front of it, will usually not require any animation by an effects animator but will be done by the layout department and painted by the background department. A prop like a cart that a character may push around will need to be animated by an effects animator. It may also have inanimate objects in it or another character, such as a monkey or a guinea pig. This would require an effects animator to draw and animate it. This would need to be done again in the rough character animation stage and would be passed back and forth between the character and effects departments for registration issues (see Figure 12.47).

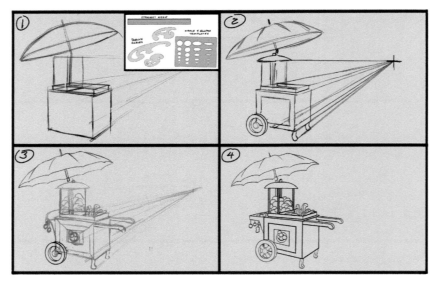

FIG 12.47 Perspective makes for strong drawing.

Let's review a scenario in which the effects department would lead the shot—in other words, a scenario where the effects have to be done first, before the character can be animated. For a scene that has an airplane doing acrobatic maneuvers while flying around in the sky, with the character visible in the cockpit, the plane would need to be animated first by an effects animator and then sent on to the character department. This would be a case of the effects animator plotting the maneuvers that the plane would make, as well as making extensive thumbnails of the action with the twists and rolls called for in the directions. This would be completed as rough animation using a simple model (1). The second pass would be with a tighter drawing of the animated plane minus the propeller, saving that element for the final pass in the animation. The propeller would be done as a series of speed lines and faint multiple images of the propeller (see Figure 12.48).

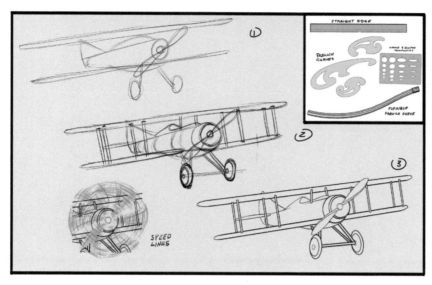

FIG 12.48 Stages of prop animation.

A hand-drawn cart would need collaborative interaction between the character and effects animators. Here the character animator would lead, indicating a rough cart he would animate, probably registering the hands, with just the handles. To be done right, though, the rough character animation would need to go to the effects animator for rough cart animation before character cleanup. It might be argued that the scene could go directly to cleanup after the character animation was roughed out, but registration errors would be inevitable and then the scene would need to go back to cleanup for revisions. Better to do it right the first time and save time in the overall production pipeline (see Figure 12.49).

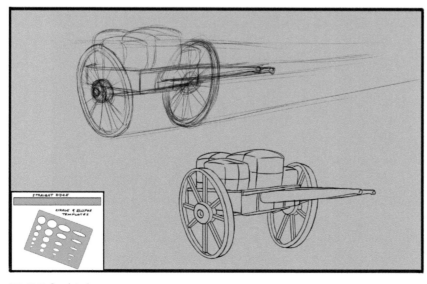

FIG 12.49 Rough to clean up prop.

A handheld candle could be handled by the character cleanup department if the candlestick placeholder that they used was drawn consistently without too many volume variations, but it's very easy for inconsistencies to occur as the hand is moving. Usually the cleanup artists are careful when doing something like this if they are reminded of the problems that may occur and stay vigilant to the potential dilemmas (see Figure 12.50).

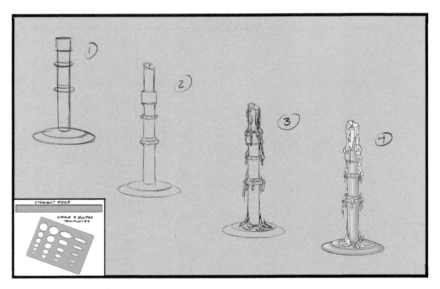

FIG 12.50 Consistency in drawing.

Communication between departments is always the best resource to solve problems before they occur. No one wants to redo work that they have spent a great deal of time and effort on. The more facts and possible problems that are shared between departments, the smoother the production. The "brain trust" is a meeting where department heads and the art director get together to discuss each sequence in the storyboard stage of a film before it goes into production. In this meeting, they solve problems before they become problems and usually find solutions to those problems through a combined effort. So talk it up, folks! Don't be shy about pointing out something you may not understand or find questionable. Try to have a solution to a problem, rather than just problems!

CHAPTER 13

Trees, Leaves, and Grass

I believe a leaf of grass is no less than the journey-work of the stars.

—Walt Whitman

Animating leaves—on trees, falling from a tree, or the ones on the ground that take flight when the wind blows—can be handled in several different ways. Let's start with a weeping willow tree, with its long runners. The design and detail depends on the background. Keep them simple if you can! Animate them in two separate layers. The runners on the backside (1) of the tree could be painted by the background department or as a held drawing done by the effects animator. Anchor the tendrils at varying heights somewhere within the middle of the tree using random irregular guides (2), so you will animate runners that are assorted in length. Animate these levels of runners with slightly offset timing from each other, in long sweeping arcs, flowing back and forth with overlapping action as the wind gusts.

Animate one level at a time so that your timing on Level 1 is not exactly like the second level (3). When you composite all the levels together, they should have a natural look to it (4) (see Figure 13.1).

The animation of the runners should be slow and lazy to accentuate the droopy feeling of the long runners, unless otherwise directed (see Figure 13.2).

Leaves covering a tree such as an oak tree should be animated as a series of clusters. These clusters will animate independently of each other but will sway in unison to the wind. The timing of the clusters can be offset from one another by two or three frames as they sway to the dictates of the wind. Animating these individual clusters will be easier than trying to animate the entire tree all as one unit.

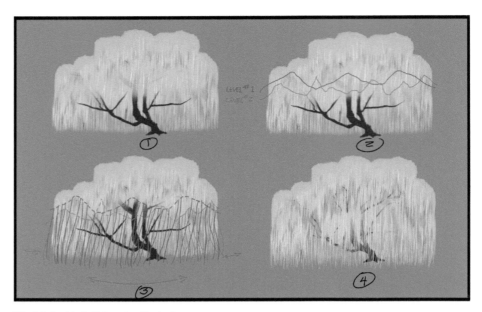

FIG 13.1 Combine held elements with animates ones.

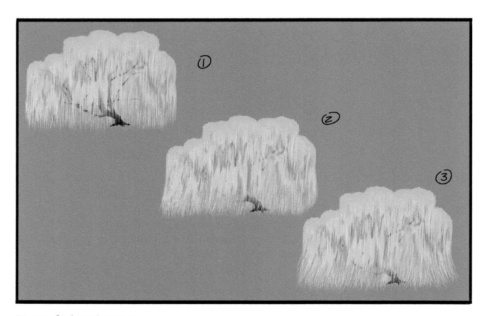

FIG 13.2 Gentle swaying actions.

Determine the clusters before you start animating (1). Keep the animation simple! This is an oak tree and very sturdy, so don't go overboard. Overlap the swaying clusters as you animate (2, 3) (see Figure 13.3).

A cypress tree, with its thick layers of rounded woody cones and small scalelike leaves, will move almost as one unit. The small, flattened shoots may separate and enhance the overall silhouette, but because of their dense foliage they will sway leisurely, with the top end moving the most (see Figure 13.4).

A palm tree will move similarly at the top end because of the fan-shaped leaves that make it so top-heavy. Although the trunk itself is very flexible, the leaves of a palm tree will lead the

FIG 13.3 Animate clusters.

FIG 13.4 Animate as one unit.

primary action of the trunk, as the leaves capture the wind, are easily influenced by its force (1), and thus will lead the action of the swaying trunk. As the trunk sways back and forth (2) to the command of the wind, the secondary actions are the leaves flapping furiously to the force of the wind (3, 4) (see Figure 13.5).

A tree as large as a sequoia tree is so massive that, although it will sway in the wind, its movement will be slight and almost imperceptible. What you will animate are the leaves and branches bobbing to the wind. The wind will move the branches slightly less than the leaves, if at all. Remember that you're dealing with a very large scale here (1). This will illustrate the scale we're working with in a sequoia tree versus the trees we've been

FIG 13.5 Overlapping layers.

looking at in this chapter (2). The leaves will animate more slowly than that oak tree because of the scale factor, so we'll only see the clusters of leaves on those branches (3, 4). They will sway up and down and side to side like a small boat bobbing on water (see Figure 13.6).

FIG 13.6 Minimal action in large scale trees.

When you animate loose leaves, whether falling from a tree being tossed in the air by children playing in a mound of raked-up leaves or just flying in the air as a story point, you want to be sure you know what they look like before you start animating them. I like to do a series of designs so that I can get familiar with how they look, as well as different varieties of leaves and color. This will help me to pick and choose the ones I plan to use so that I can simplify the designs and design them into an element that I can eventually animate with confidence, as in the following illustrations. These were done with colored pastels on black paper so that the designs would be easier to read. That's not always the best way to draw them, but it was fall and the colors were hard to resist (see Figure 13.7).

FIG 13.7 Leaf designs.

I will simplify the designs to line work for animation purposes (see Figure 13.8).

FIG 13.8 Simple line drawing.

Once the designs are set, I draw the path of action to which I will animate the leaves (see Figure 13.9).

Leaf animation path of action.

Animating bundles of leaves takes a little planning in terms of how the leaves will tumble, twist, or bend. Some will curlicue and some will meander, but the focus must be to make them all move along the same path without getting overly complex in their patterns (see Figure 13.10).

FIG 13.10 Animate group of leaves along a path.

Keep it simple and animate some leaves tumbling and some just floating along, some twisting and others simply flapping. Mix them up within the batches of floating leaves. Animate a few as separate levels and composite them later. Keep the overall flow following and stretching out over your established path of action (see Figure 13.11).

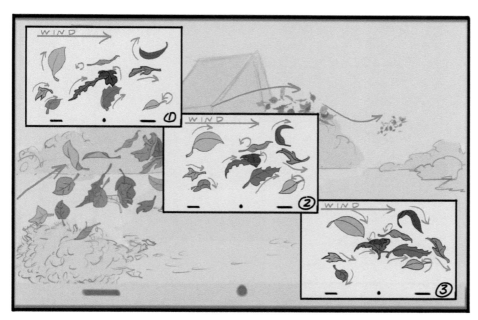

FIG 13.11 Vary the individual leaf animation.

Animate the leaves following the path as they travel and thin out over time, with some stragglers overlapping the action from behind the main body of the leaves as they disappear into the distance (see Figure 13.12).

FIG 13.12 Leaf animation.

A leaf floating lazily from a tree can be animated more easily if you use a figure eight path of action to describe the path of action it will be traveling (see Figure 13.13).

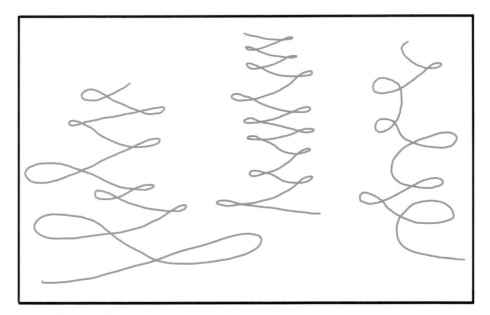

FIG 13.13 Figure eight of action.

The figure eight paths can be delineated in a number of ways and with a number of leaf elements in a shot as they float from the tree to the ground (see Figure 13.14).

FIG 13.14 Animate a leaf through the path of action.

Let's move on to animating grass! We'll begin by animating a cycle of a group of grass leaves, simple overlapping action on all the individual grass strands moving side to side. This is a technique that will lead to filling a field with animated grass. Here is how you can accomplish this effect, by using a minimal amount of work and working smart (see Figure 13.15).

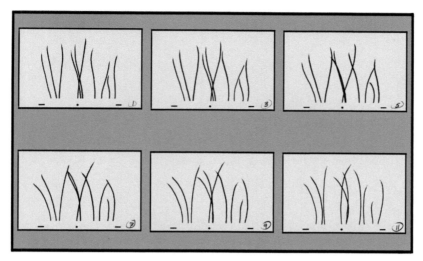

FIG **13.15** Grass cycle animation.

After you've finalized your grass animation cycle, you will need to copy the cycle and expose it as two separate levels on your exposure sheet with instructions to offset them side by side when composited and flopped (mirror image) not only to offset your timing but also to add volume to the grass level and keep it from looking too similar. Give the camera department through the scene planning department very specific instructions, along with your phone number or extension so that the scene planning department can call you if they need to clarify (see Figure 13.16).

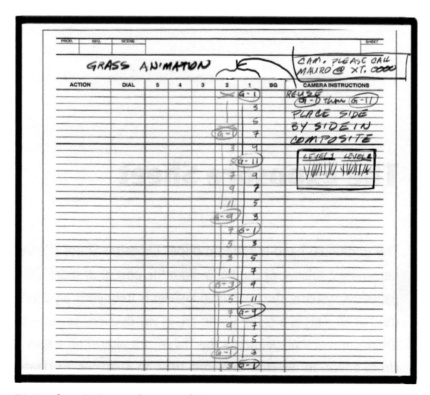

FIG **13.16** Grass animation exposed on exposure sheet.

Have an illustration for the scene planning and camera departments to show them how you want the composite animation to look (see Figure 13.17).

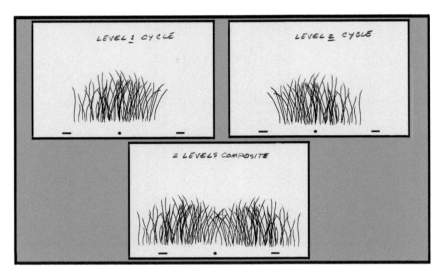

FIG **13.17** Compositing 2 groups of grass animation.

The next step in your instructions would be to have scene planning combine the composites of the grass at varying heights (red lines) to get a sense of depth and mass for your final composite. Composite Level 3 behind Composite Level 2 and both behind Composite Level 1. The completed composite, using as many levels needed to accumulate the desired mass by using the composite levels at varying heights, may look like this (Level 4)—as dense or as sparse as is required or desired (see Figure 13.18).

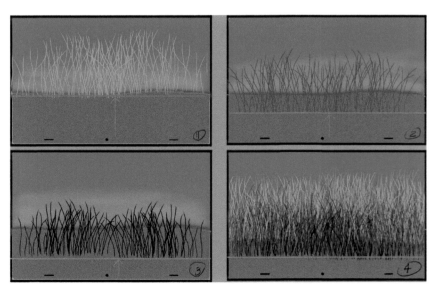

FIG **13.18** Layering your composite.

The same technique can be used to animate large-scale grasses such as pampas grass. The following array illustrates how to use the feathery heads to animate the broader overlap and drag of the pampas grass (see Figure 13.19).

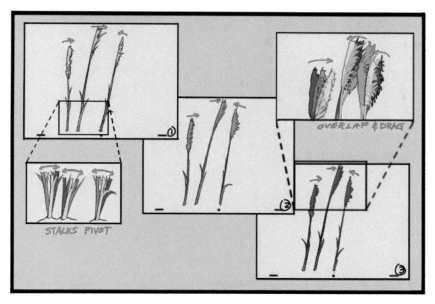

FIG 13.19 Pampas grass animation.

Even though the stalks are more rigid and don't bend much, they have a gentle sway. The tough stalks sway back and forth, pivoting from their bases securely planted in the ground. I would suggest animating the stalks first, describing a nice smooth arc of motion as they sway back and forth. In this example, I'll just draw nine stalks moving right to left (see Figure 13.20).

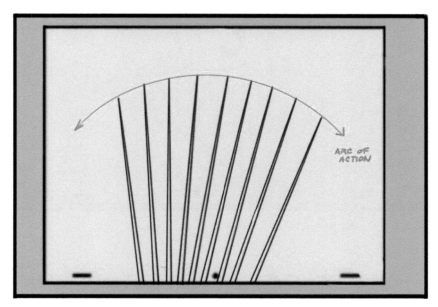

FIG 13.20 Animate the stalk first.

Once I've got a smooth arc on the stalk, I can animate the feathery head in a move from right to left. First design the fluffy head with some clear shapes that can be animated in overlapping action as the grass sways left (see Figure 13.21).

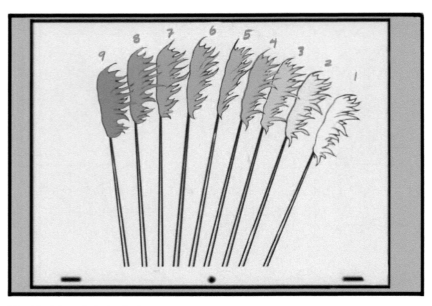

FIG 13.21 Animate the feathery heads.

Next I'll finish the animation of the same element, changing direction left to right, and complete the cycle of the swaying pampas grass (see Figure 13.22).

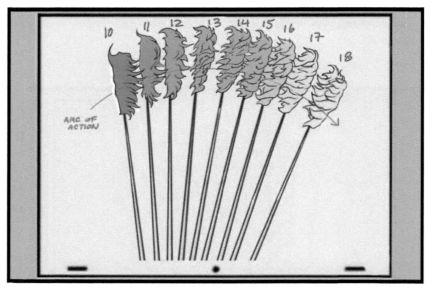

FIG 13.22 Complete the animation cycle.

Overlapping action, drag, and follow-through are some of the basic principle actions to describe the animation taking place here in this chapter, whether it's a tree swaying back and forth or a blade of grass.

CHAPTER 14

Pixie Dust, Mattes, and Slot Gags

We come spinning out of nothingness, scattering stars like dust.

—Rumi

Pixie dust is often associated with faeries and magical effects moments. Here are a number of ways to animate those elements, as well as some other uses for "pixie dust" or "sparkles" in some common scenarios. When animating pixie dust, I first roughly block out the area or the path that will be pixie dust behind the object or character that's emitting the dust with the side of my pencil. I do this because it's best to animate this effect as straight-ahead animation. The rough is a great substructure to work from and gives the animator latitude to make changes if he or she wishes (see Figure 14.1).

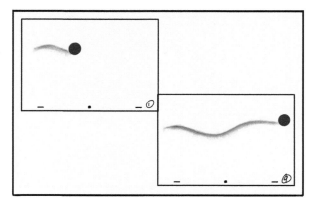

FIG 14.1 Animate rough path of action using side of pencil.

The way I plan it, the darker areas in the final roughs will have a higher concentration of the pixie dust, usually at the base of the rough where all the pixie dust will naturally gravitate as it falls (see Figure 14.2).

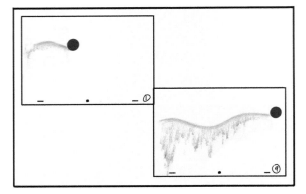

FIG 14.2 Complete rough animation.

It won't be necessary to follow every dot in your animation. The heavier concentration of the particles are what you will be following, and then only in terms of maintaining the volumes that will eventually thin out as the effect evolves (see Figure 14.3).

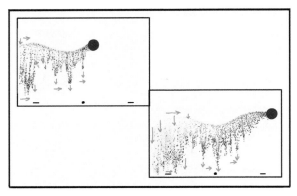

FIG 14.3 Animate the particles on top of rough.

A few of the larger pixie dust particles can lead the animation as well as drag behind, anchoring the effect to the path of action. Those are the particles that you will definitely follow and dissolve off as you animate. The particles are black against white paper but will be processed in reverse and become white or whatever color necessary (image 15) (see Figure 14.4).

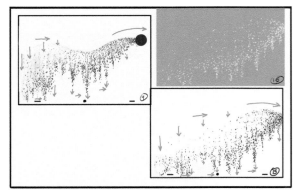

FIG 14.4 Particle animation.

If you are animating a medium or close-up shot of pixie dust, when you complete the main body of the pixie dust, you should go back to the beginning of your shot and add some sparkly highlights throughout your animation, as a separate level. These sparkle effect highlights are usually optional on long shots (see Figure 14.5).

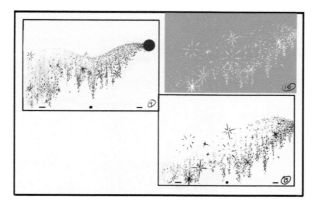

FIG **14.5** Add sparkle animation.

The pixie dust can be used as a projectile type of effect that bursts on impact, similar to fireworks, but will hit its intended target and expand quickly, then form some concentrated clusters and fall lightly (see Figure 14.6).

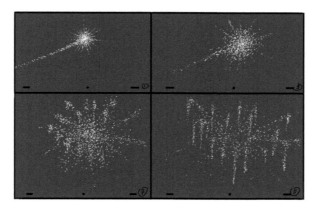

FIG **14.6** Pixie dust animation 1.

It will dissipate as it falls (see Figure 14.7).

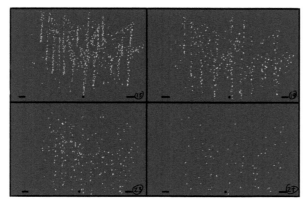

FIG **14.7** Pixie dust animation 2.

A simple burst of dust would start with a high concentration of dots that expand quickly, radiate out, and then quickly fade by simply diminishing the number of dots with each succeeding drawing (see Figure 14.8).

FIG 14.8 Pixie dust bursts.

The added "pixie sparkles" can have some variations in how they animate (see Figure 14.9). Some simply pop on and fade off (1) in one place, some pop on then twist back and forth and pop off (2) in place, while some pop on and "float" up and down slightly before they pop off or fade off (3). Lastly, some will fade on and fade off as they twist (4) and float around the body of pixie dust around them. You can have these sparkles on for 12 or 18 frames if you so choose, as long as it fits within the timing of the dust around them. Here are some of the timing variations that I like to use in medium and close-up shots.

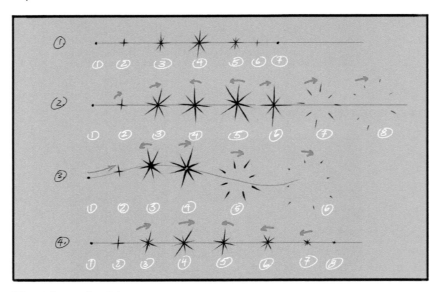

FIG 14.9 Some sparkle variations.

Sparks can be used to highlight or enhance other types of effects, such as sparks from a train braking (see Figure 14.10).

FIG 14.10 Sparks from train breaking.

These can be easily animated in five to six frame cycles coming off the braking system on the steel wheels, using streaks and sparks of several different colors (see Figure 14.11).

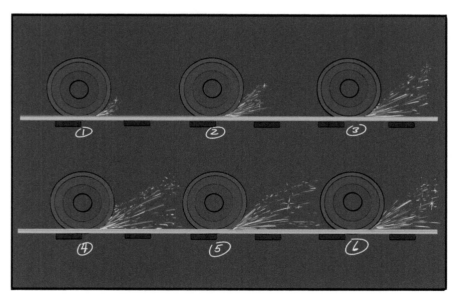

FIG 14.11 Sparks cycle animation.

Sparks that occur when an electrical outlet or light blows out last only 8 to 12 frames (see Figure 14.12).

Traditional spark effect animation was used as squibs in live-action films, such as science fiction films—for example, when a laser beam misses its target and ricochets, striking a wall or a prop that then goes flying off its resting place. Squibs may last three to four frames!

FIG 14.12 Electrical sparks.

There are many uses for such a simple effect, and when used correctly it can be just enough to sell the effect as realistic (see Figure 14.13).

FIG 14.13 Squibs animation.

Magical effects, such as something a wizard may conjure up in his hands, may have a variety of effects as well as sparkles. And then the wizard sends a fiendish bolt of energy from his hands (see Figure 14.14).

FIG 14.14 Magical effects animation.

There is a more mechanical method to animate "sparkles," such as the glints you see as the sun reflects off the surface of the water of a lake or the ocean. Animating the sparkles by hand is labor-intensive and really not necessary, when the same effect can be accomplished by the use of a few simple mattes and some camera work. Here's what the animation camera setup looks like (see Figure 14.15).

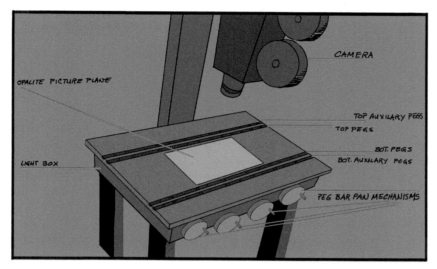

FIG 14.15 Animation down-shooter camera.

Let's start with a simple background of a sunset over water (see Figure 14.16).

FIG 14.16 Background.

The illusion is to make it look as if the water is moving even though the background is a still painted image. If the sunlight looks like it's glittering on the surface of the water, then you are making the audience believe they are seeing movement on the water. You can achieve this effect quite easily with the use of a few simple mattes and some thinking and planning on your part! Make a negative matte by tracing the highlight on the water on a blank sheet of paper, then transfer it onto a black sheet of paper that has top peg registration (A) that masks all except the parts of the highlights on the background (see Figure 14.17).

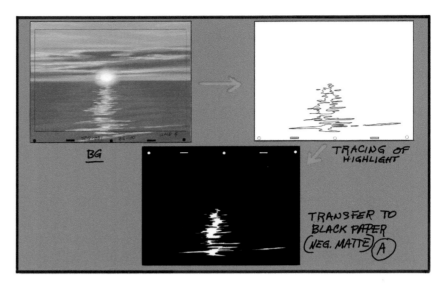

FIG 14.17 Slot gag negative matte.

A *slot gag* is basically two levels of perforated black paper; when shot on a down-shooter or animation camera rig, with a bottom light on, the light will show through the perforations of the black paper. So this next part calls for a little work on your part. On a separate sheet of *black paper with the peg holes on top,* cut vertical slits of varying lengths with a sharp blade from the left to right sides (B). Make the slits thick enough that light can shine through, but not much wider that the blade.

On the second piece of black paper, make horizontal cuts of varying lengths, top to bottom (C). The *peg holes should be on the bottom of the paper* on this one and it will work with the bottom peg bar on the camera tabletop (see Figure 14.18).

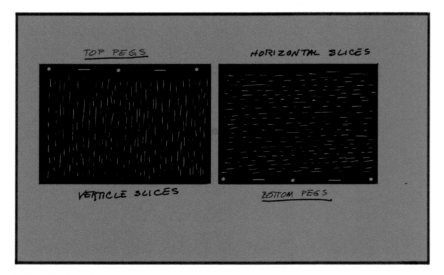

FIG 14.18 Slot gag elements.

Now assemble all your elements on the down-shooter, starting with the *negative matte (A) on the top peg bars,* the bottom light on, and the top lights off. The idea here is that the clear area that allows the bottom light to shine through will be the only area that will be affected in the background, and the rest is protected and will remain as originally painted (see Figure 14.19).

FIG 14.19 Negative matte of light table.

Lay the black paper with the vertical slots (B) on the *top auxiliary pegs* so that this level will move in increments equal to, but in the opposite direction of, the horizontal slots (C) on the *bottom pegs* and independent of the regular top pegs that hold Level A (see Figure 14.20).

FIG 14.20 Slot gag elements on top of matte.

Only the light that is allowed to shine through the negative matte (A) will affect the slots cut into the black papers. Because of the random way in which they were cut, the light will come and go just as randomly and create an effect of pinpoints of light bouncing off the water surface. Some will linger longer than others, but all will be exposed only in the contained area of the negative matte (A) (see Figure 14.21).

FIG 14.21 Light shines through slots.

The finished slot gag effects element will look something like this and be ready for composite to the background (see Figure 14.22).

FIG 14.22 Slot gag effect element.

When the slot gag effect is finally composited with the background element, this is the effect that you'll get. There are some options open to you as you shoot this effect on camera. First, you can shoot this effect with a colored gel on the lens to match the colors that are prevalent in the background painting. Another option is to use a filter on the lens, such as a starlight filter. This will mimic the effect of squinting when looking at a bright light source, resulting in the pin lights flaring and causing starlike effects on the water. Lastly, some diffusion will soften the effect and may add a feeling of depth if you apply it to the lower portions of the image (see Figure 14.23).

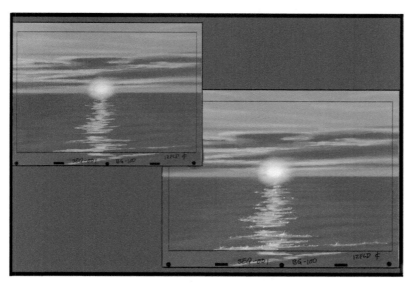

FIG 14.23 Composit on background.

Now, what exactly are mattes? Mattes are useful in blocking areas that you wish to protect and keep from altering or pinpoint areas that you wish to affect and alter. Here's how. I'll use a background that is finished as one solid level without any overlays or any separate levels in it for my example for the use of mattes (see Figure 14.24).

FIG 14.24 Background.

The director thinks that the village looks too unoccupied, so directs the effects department to add some smoke coming from some of the chimneys and some lights for atmosphere. First thing to do is pick where I want to animate smoke from on the background image (see Figure 14.25).

FIG 14.25 Smoke animation.

Positive Mattes: I animate the smoke on top of the background image, picking areas from behind buildings from which the smoke will emanate. I then make *positive or holdout mattes* in these areas (see Figure 14.26).

FIG 14.26 Smoke animation composited.

By articulating the edges of these mattes as precisely as possible around the background image, I will cover the area where the smoke will look to be behind something, giving the shot the sense that the smoke is rising from behind a building or a chimney or even in the midst of a group of buildings, while allowing me to animate freely knowing that the animation will be clipped by the matte edges (see Figure 14.27).

Now I can treat the smoke as I like and composite it on the background (see Figure 14.28).

The last thing to do now is accomplish the director's final directive of adding lights for atmosphere to the background. This will be done by using negative mattes.

FIG 14.27 Smoke animation and mattes.

FIG 14.28 Smoke animation.

Negative Mattes: These mattes block everything within the frame that you do not wish to alter or affect, allowing you to maintain the integrity of the image or images covered by the black areas. The open space, or the *negative matte*, will allow you to alter only those areas within the confines of those open areas. In this case, the negative matte will give you the ability to change the color values of the background without changing the color, or as in this case it will lighten those areas, making it appear that there are light sources being brightened.

First we'll add lights in some of the windows by tracing some of those windows from the background buildings and transferring their positions onto black paper by painting those areas white against the black (see Figure 14.29).

FIG 14.29 Negative mattes of windows.

These window mattes will be exposed as lighter areas on the background, as lights coming from within the buildings. But there's still something missing, so we'll do some other negative mattes to be treated a little differently against the background.

These next negative mattes will simulate lanterns on the outside of the buildings and the light cast from them. We'll do these a bit different this time. These mattes, although they are hard-edged, will eventually be blurred and diffused, making these areas look like soft light cast from the lanterns. We will also make some negative mattes for their reflection in the water and highlighted areas on the walls and boats that may catch some of the ambient light (see Figure 14.30).

FIG 14.30 Soft negative mattes of reflections.

Once these negative mattes are blurred and diffused, they will look like this (see Figure 14.31).

FIG 14.31 Negative mattes blurred and diffused.

Now we will combine the windows and lantern negative mattes and see what we get from all our work (see Figure 14.32).

FIG 14.32 Negative mattes: composite element.

Once we composite all our effects elements together, our final image should have the look that the director envisioned (see Figure 14.33).

FIG 14.33 Final composite.

Now, before my background friends start raising a ruckus, I should explain that this "fix" would normally be done by the background painter. I just used this example to demonstrate how positive and negative mattes can be utilized.

Positive and negative mattes can also be used in unison and will produce varied results depending on the desired orientation (see Figures 14.34 and 14.35).

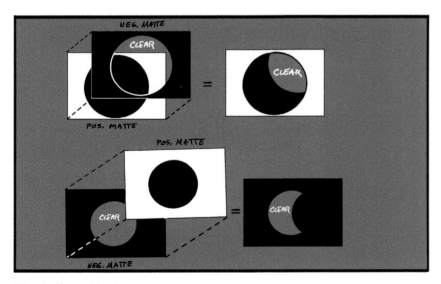

FIG 14.34 Matte variations 1.

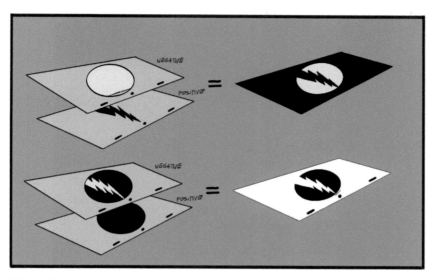

FIG 14.35 Matte variations 2.

CHAPTER 15

Fantasy Effects and Ectoplasm

Tell me where is Fancy bred, or in the heart or in the head?

—Shakespeare

Ectoplasm and fantasy or fanciful effects are often the representative images affiliated or analogous to ghosts, poltergeists, or some other supernatural creatures. They can be benevolent or benign creatures but also cruel, spiteful, or malevolent brutes.

Ectoplasm in its purest or simplest form is just amorphous shapes that can be animated as one or more shape that can be interwoven as they rise from the floor or emerge from a wall or prop. The element would be painted with interior colors to give the effect body and texture (see Figure 15.1).

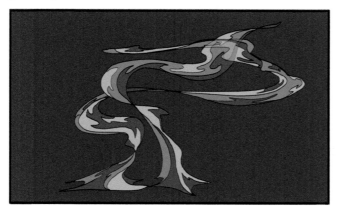

FIG 15.1 Raw ectoplasm animation.

Once the animation is complete, the next step must be to treat the element, usually with blur, diffusion, and opacity, to fit properly into the setting and interact with the props or some other effect you may add (see Figure 15.2).

FIG 15.2 Treated ectoplasm animation.

Most of these shapes or creatures are conjured up from the imagination of a writer, but it is the artist who must match an image to the writer's descriptions. The artist's imagination can flourish and breathe life into some very imaginative creations. But we must always be cognizant of how the effects need to be treated and broken down to be able to accomplish the desired effect, like a melting zombie (see Figure 15.3).

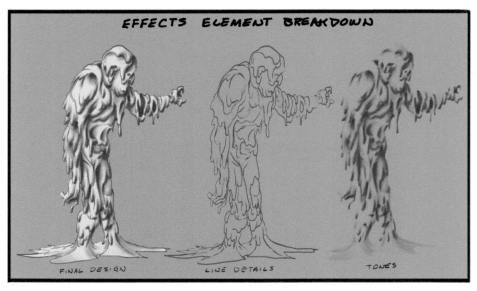

FIG 15.3 Effects: creature element.

No matter the effect element, always be mindful of how you will achieve that final look. Try variations of placement of layers and the treatment of each with its partner layers (see Figure 15.4).

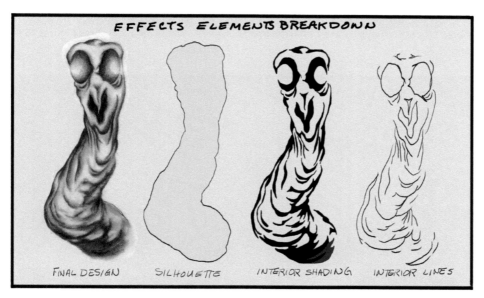

FIG 15.4 Effects: element breakdown.

There are times when research can help, but you need only to look around for inspiration and can extract designs from everyday objects that can inspire images of frightening forms and creatures. Twisted gnarly tree roots or vines always fascinate me and I photograph them constantly, as well as rocks and even shapes formed from spilled liquids! I'm constantly on the lookout for things that may be of interest. Here are some possibilities (see Figure 15.5).

FIG 15.5 Photo references.

Use your imagination to extract some images and then try to use them in their most appropriate circumstances or context. Once the design is finalized, you need to break down the sum of their parts in order to figure out what it will take to animate it, the number of levels necessary to make it, and how best to treat them to accomplish the desired look. As in some of the following cases, sometimes you may even see more than one vision in the same object! Cross your eyes, stare, or flip the image around—whatever it takes (see Figures 15.6 and 15.7).

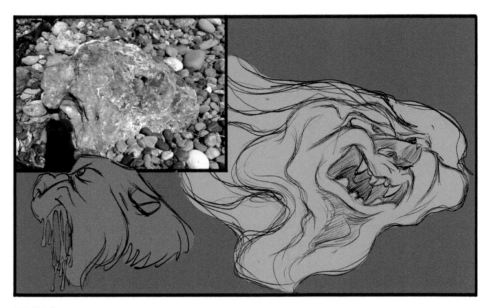

FIG 15.6 Fantasy creatures.

FIG 15.7 Fantasy creatures from gnarly branches.

Don't be afraid to let your imagination run wild. It may be something you pick up at first glance that may not make sense at first, but start roughing out quickly and worry about the details later (see Figure 15.8).

FIG 15.8 Impressions from photographs.

It can start with seeing an eye in an open space, and then one thing may lead to another. Don't give up on it. You never know where it will end up (see Figure 15.9).

FIG 15.9 Creates creatures from inspiring photos.

The image may or may not be obvious when you first see it, but how and where you can use it will be your biggest challenge. Even if you can't use it for your current project, put it away in your files and save it for future projects. It may end up that you'll never use it again, but what you learn from it will stay stored in that depository you call a brain until some future event sparks a memory (see Figure 15.10).

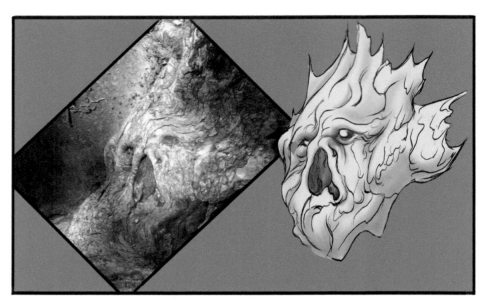

FIG 15.10 There's inspiration everywhere.

The stupidest doodle can suddenly jump off your blank piece of paper in your sketch book. So don't discard anything right away. You may be able to nurture and develop it to something great or some silly nonsense! Don't take anything for granted. Good or bad, you may find a use for it! (see Figure 15.11).

FIG 15.11 Use texture to inspire.

This particular effect started out being some sharp scribbles on a scrap piece of paper that I worked up into an effect (see Figure 15.12).

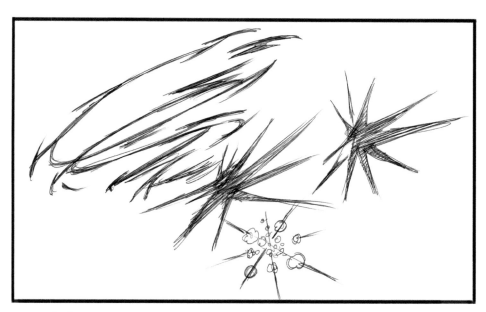

FIG 15.12 Doodles.

I reworked and refined it a bit as an effect from which a faerie emerges from some sparkling reflections (see Figure 15.13).

FIG 15.13 Fantasy effect.

The point here is to never stop experimenting. I can't stress this enough! The more you draw, the easier it will be for you to create. Doodle away, and look for interesting shapes and images all around you that can spark your imagination!

CHAPTER 16

Lava and Mud

It is the lava of the imagination, whose eruption prevents an earthquake.

—*Lord Byron*

Technically, lava is only called *lava* once magma flows from beneath the surface to above ground. Lava has a much greater viscosity than water, even though it can flow in the same manner.

When lava stops moving, it turns solid and forms igneous rock. Lava is made up of different percentages of chemicals such as iron, aluminum, silica, potassium, sodium, calcium, and magnesium, as well as others. Lava moves with a casual deliberateness and an undeniable destructive force. Even though it may move in a lethargic manner sometimes, it is a juggernaut that is nearly unstoppable. It can creep along at a steady pace like globs of ever-stretching taffy, layers that fold over layers, or fluid-like water rushing down a gorge!

If I'm going to animate lava rushing down a canyon, I first want to rough out the path of action it will take. It may come into contact with obstructions like a cliff face or a large rock outcropping in the middle of its path, so I need to plan for a wave of lava crashing against the cliff or a change in its flow as it sweeps around the obstruction or flows over it to cover it entirely. I treat it pretty much like rapids rushing down a river. Plan for eddies or swirls that may occur as the flow dictates. I can vary the timing as I move forward with the animation.

Here's an example to illustrate how I may approach a scene I'm describing, making sure that my perspective is true to the background using a grid (see Figure 16.1).

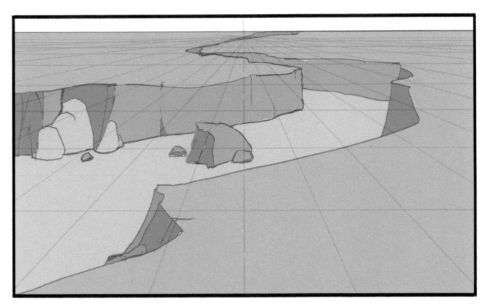

FIG 16.1 Background with perspective grid.

Now I'll draw my rough flow animation following the path of the gorge in the background (see Figure 16.2).

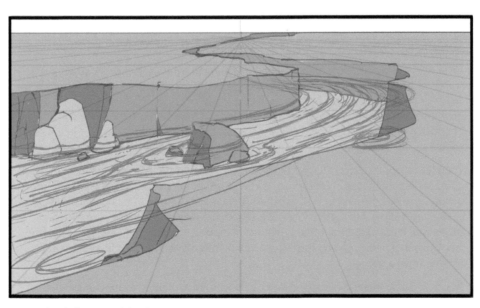

FIG 16.2 Lava buffering around obstacles.

Using my rough flow animation as a guide, I will make a positive matte of the area of the lava in the gorge, painting it black to represent the surface crust of the flow. I leave negative line spaces within the matte that would follow the lava flow from the rough drawing in varying line thicknesses that would make it fit within the scale of the landscape. I mimic the cracks on the crust's surface (see Figure 16.3).

FIG 16.3 Top level of lava (crust).

Next, I need to make a negative matte to make certain that only the area I want to be affected is isolated and the rest of the background is protected. Tracing the silhouette of the positive matte precisely assures me that my negative matte will be accurate (see Figure 16.4).

FIG 16.4 Negative matte.

To mimic the underlying lava flow beneath the black crust, I paint a broad area covering the area the positive matte encompasses, using intense shades of red, orange, and yellow. This will work as a separate level and will be exposed under the positive matte level (see Figure 16.5).

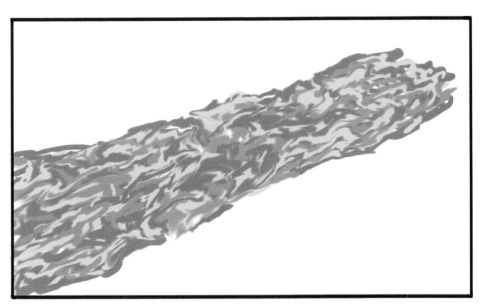

FIG 16.5 Color level.

By panning the color level diagonally slowly and at the same angle as the gorge, it will portray the lava flow. At this distance in the background and scale, it would look to move slowly, so a slow pan would be called for (see Figure 16.6).

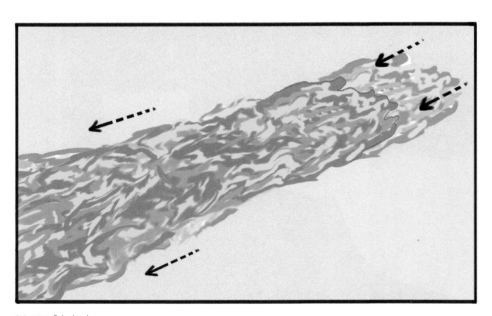

FIG 16.6 Color level pan.

By exposing the negative matte on top of the color level as it pans, I will be sure to have the color level captured only within the negative space and covering only the area of the positive matte and nowhere else (see Figure 16.7).

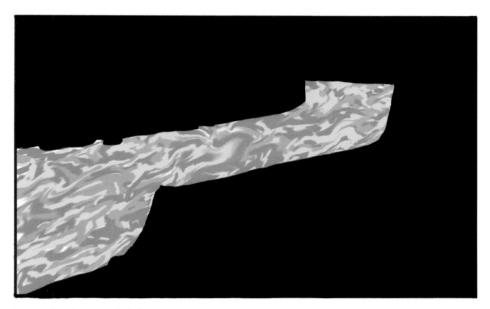

FIG 16.7 Negative matte and color level.

When all the elements are exposed together, the colors will show through the negative or open lines of the positive matte (see Figure 16.8).

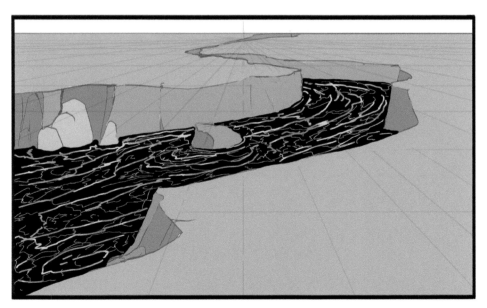

FIG 16.8 Positive matte and color level.

The addition of a level of airbrushed glows exposed on top of the crust level over the cracks will add just the right finishing touches to the scene (see Figure 16.9).

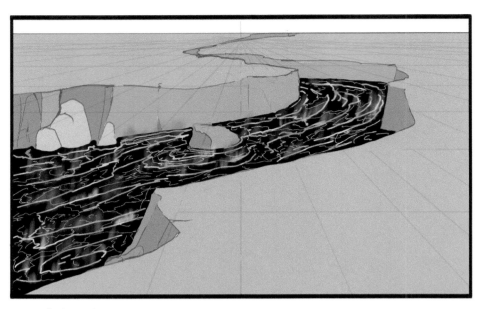

FIG 16.9 Final composite.

It may be fast-moving and have the same fluid characteristics as water does, due to the intense heat liquefying the lava, but it has a much higher viscosity. This means that the "splashes" of lava that may hit other surfaces will stick there (see Figure 16.10).

FIG 16.10 Fast-moving lava.

It can flow thick and ponderously over a landscape, creeping along hot and deadly, eradicating everything it touches under a layer of a black, crumbling surface embers of steaming hot slag (see Figure 16.11).

FIG 16.11 Lava striking obstacles.

The way I would break it down would be to use three layers. The first is the topmost level or the detailed level in black outline (see Figure 16.12).

FIG 16.12 Detailed top level.

The next two levels are rough color levels that will add dimension to the effect. I rough out the second level by articulating the silhouette of the top level (Figure 16.12). This is basically a blobby mass with rough openings throughout. This level will eventually be painted red and act as the under layer to the detailed black outline.

The next level is a copy of the second layer (Figure 16.13). It will be painted a solid yellow and will show through the rough openings of the red (see Figure 16.14).

FIG 16.13 Lava level with negative openings.

FIG 16.14 Bottom most lava level.

My next level would be a shadow element to help anchor my lava effect to the landscape (see Figure 16.15).

When the three levels are composited together, it looks like red-hot flowing lava glowing under the top level of black slag, punctuated with hot spots of yellow. Sparks thrown off by the leading edges of the lava and on its surface are added as another level of effects along with the level of leading edge of shadow under the entire composite to marry it to the ground plane (see Figure 16.16).

FIG 16.15 Shadow level and sparks.

FIG 16.16 All levels composited.

I will also add fire and smoke—a layer of smoke painted solid white and flames animated on top of the lava (see Figure 16.17).

The smoke and fire levels will then be blurred and added on top of the lava for the final composite (see Figure 16.18).

A slower flowing lava will layer itself over and over, forming stair-like formations as it does. For this type of lava, I will animate a level of thick, wavelike patterns that overlap themselves (see Figure 16.19).

FIG 16.17 Smoke and fire levels.

FIG 16.18 Final composit.

FIG 16.19 Thick lava flow.

My next layer will animate beneath the detailed wave patterns. This layer will have two to three color separations that will have the lines blurred so they will blend together, giving this level a smooth, blended look (see Figure 16.20).

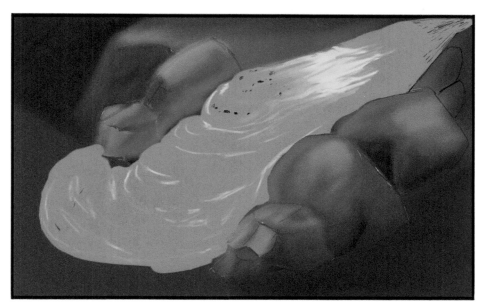

FIG 16.20 Blende lava colors.

Figure 16.21 shows what it looks like when these levels are combined.

FIG 16.21 Combined lava levels.

There are bubbling cauldrons of lava that bubble in the same manner as hot, steaming water does. As it bubbles, it shoots out small jets of lava, leaping across its surface (see Figure 16.22).

FIG 16.22 Lava bubbles.

The jets of lava burst upward, arc across the surface, and blend back into the overall flow (see Figures 16.23 through 16.25).

FIG 16.23 Lava bursts 1.

FIG 16.24 Lava bursts 2.

FIG 16.25 Lava bursts 3.

The overall lava surface may be a black mass inundated with hot fissures of steam that follow behind as the lava bubbles upward (see Figure 16.26).

I would treat the cracks on the surface with steam and or flame elements rising from those openings to accentuate the heat and deadly material beneath (see Figure 16.27).

FIG 16.26 Add steam fissures.

FIG 16.27 Steam and flame elements.

The explosive bursts of lava spraying the sides of a caldera, however, will stick to the sides, cooling and building mass (see Figure 16.28).

The lava splashes up against the side walls of the caldera (see Figure 16.29).

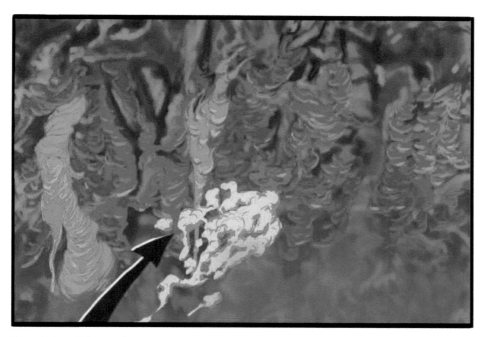

FIG **16.28** Lava splashes on walls.

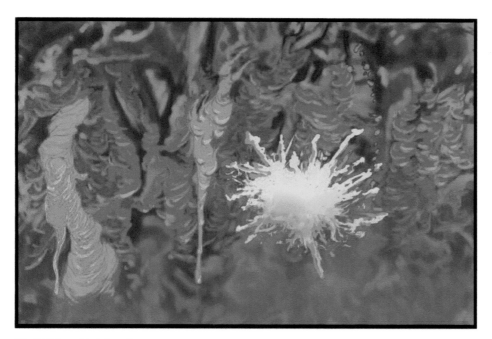

FIG **16.29** Lava sticks to the walls.

It spreads and dribbles down as it cools over the smooth sides, fusing with the previous splatters (see Figure 16.30).

The now-cooled-down splatter binds itself to the sides, building up the caldera sides layer after layer (see Figures 16.31 and 16.32).

FIG 16.30 The splashes stick to sides.

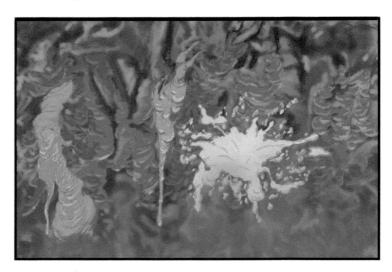

FIG 16.31 Lava builds up.

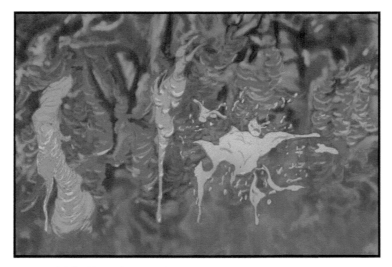

FIG 16.32 Splashes blend with existing splats.

Steam and smoke rise from the superheated lava and ash along with the slag floating on top. Here are two examples of how to animate the smoke rising up out of the fissures in the conflagration of a lava flow. First animate two, one thin and the other broader (A and B), or three levels of thin smoke (D, E, and F), then combine them, diffusing each, altering the opacity of one or all to blend them as they intertwine and they rise (C and G). These serve as good background elements, adding depth to the setting (see Figure 16.33).

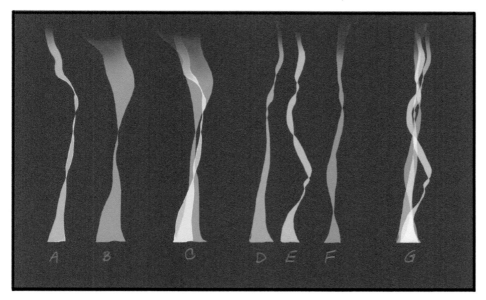

FIG 16.33 Smoke combinations.

Superheated steam shoots up in a jet-like manner and then dissipates once it reaches its maximum height. Using a dry brush technique or speed lines to mimic a compacted stream of steam, combined with a tight volume of spray, animate the two elements as one. The effects shoots up quickly out of an opening or even a small explosive burst of lava (see Figures 16.34 and 16.35).

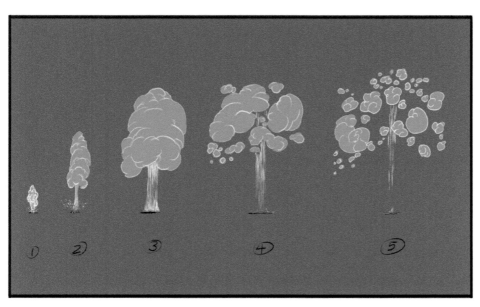

FIG 16.34 Steam animation.

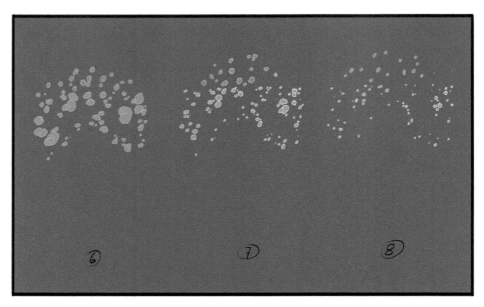

FIG 16.35 Steam dissipating.

Here's another example of steam animation. This one is more cursive after its initial breach, discharging a fog of vapor that then floats upward (see Figure 16.36).

FIG 16.36 More steam animation.

It will then disperse high above in sinuous, snakelike streams (see Figure 16.37).

Mud is the result of a mixture of water and earth. The texture can be sludgy, oozy, silty, sticky, soft, fine-grained, or coarse. It will spatter on a body, clothes, or shoes. Mud can flow in a liquefied state, or it can be quite thick and heavy. In its liquid state, it can flow in a slurry-like manner (see Figure 16.38).

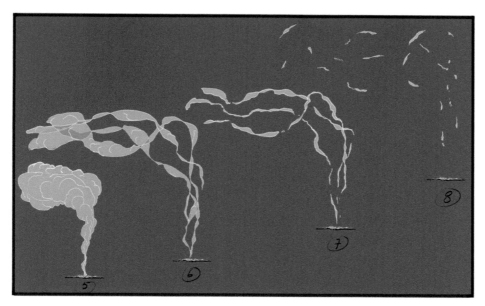

FIG **16.37** Steam dissipating.

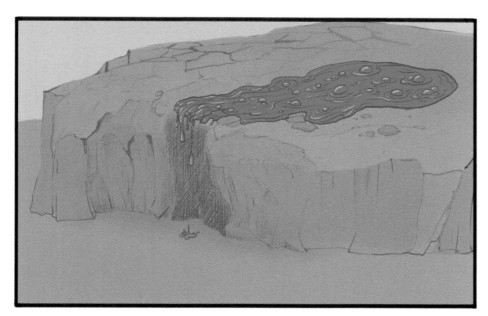

FIG **16.38** Mud slurry.

The consistency is watery with some bubbles and lumps of heavier material floating within the stream (see Figure 16.39).

Even though the mud is liquid, it moves with a sluggishness determined by its greater density and consistency. It will "plop" and "splatter" thickly and spread slowly (see Figure 16.40).

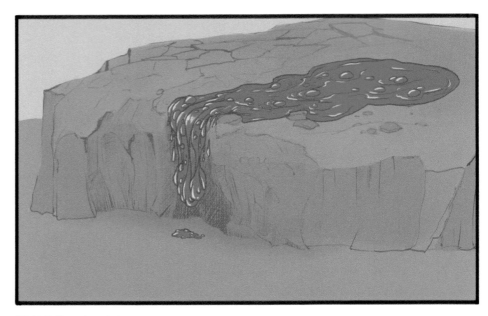

FIG 16.39 Heavy clumps in slurry.

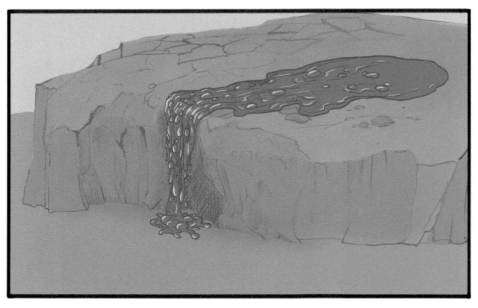

FIG 16.40 Slow thick movement.

It will bubble as it spreads, trapping air pockets within its aggregate (see Figure 16.41).

It will spread, radiating out until it cannot flow anymore, and will then start losing its moisture and start to dry out (see Figure 16.42).

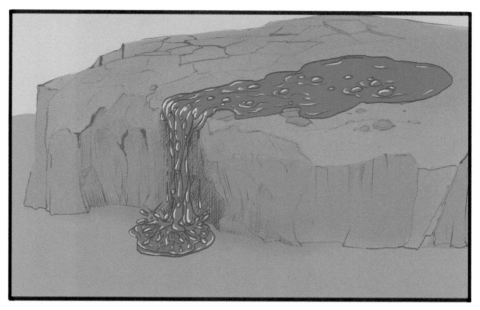

FIG 16.41 Bubbles form in the slurry.

FIG 16.42 Mud builds up and dries.

Geothermal activity underground pushes, "burps," water through mud and ash, forming small volcano-like pots of mud, popping through the surface and creating mud craters. These are called *mud pots*. Some are slight and pop up slowly with very little discharge (see Figure 16.43).

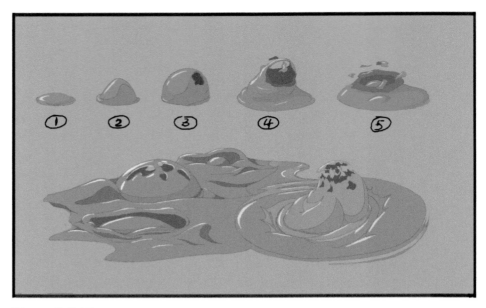

FIG 16.43 Mud bubble.

Some of these mud pots will explode with a fearsome energy, forming a variety of interesting designs as they pop! (see Figure 16.44).

FIG 16.44 Mud bubbles bursting.

Here is an example of an animated mild mud pot (see Figure 16.45).

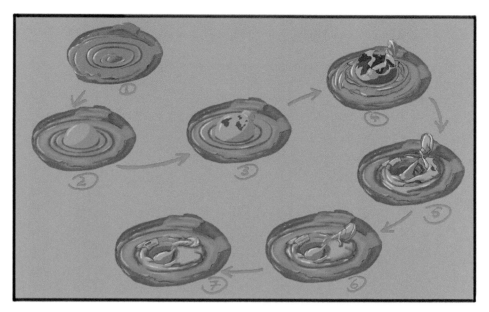

FIG 16.45 Mud bubble progression.

Here is one just quickly roughed out (see Figure 16.46).

FIG 16.46 Rust bubble burst progression.

As a bicycle rolls across a puddle of mud, it picks up mud in its treads that clings there as the tire rotates. The mud is flung from the rear of the tire in a rooster-tail pattern due to the momentum of the rotation of the tire, as well as to the sides as the wheels cut through the fluid substance. It will follow a trajectory away from the tire, arcing back to the ground in clumps and long strands of liquid streams, even as the other end clings to the tire before finally blending into the treads or being flung off (see Figure 16.47).

FIG 16.47 Mud on bicycle tires.

Clumps of mud thrown in the air will travel in an arc to their destination following the trajectory in which they were launched. A mud clump may be compacted into a ball or a cluster. Clumps of mud will leave a trail of smaller clumps as they travel behind the main body following the same arc (see Figure 16.48).

FIG 16.48 Mud clumps.

Once a clump of mud hits a wall or an intended object, it will cling, leaving a splatter pattern on its silhouette (1) and even drippings from its moisture contents (2). Mud will stick to shoes, boots, or even bare feet (3), trailing thick and slimy as someone trudges through the mucky substance (see Figure 16.49).

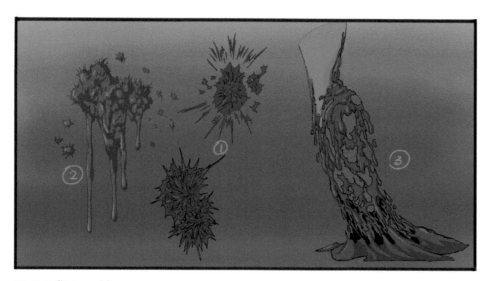

FIG 16.49 Clinging mud clumps.

CHAPTER 17

Lightning and Electricity

Thunder is good, thunder is impressive; but it's lightning that does all the work.

—*Mark Twain*

Lightning is a matter of individual style. You can follow my animating technique for lightning. Use this as groundwork to start building your own techniques. However, my best advice is to also practice a variety of techniques—to seek out your peers and especially experienced animators and ask them to demonstrate their techniques. Your lightning animation style will develop from applying the cumulative methods you study. The method I'm demonstrating is as good as any, but I would still urge you to seek other methods and styles as well. When animating lightning, timing will make or break the effect! "Snapping" from one position to the next and using the proper timing while doing it, as well as a strong design, is what your ultimate goal should be. Animate lightning on ones and straight ahead while playing the cracking sound of a lightning bolt strike in your head as you animate. It may help achieve the desired effect. Lightning can last anywhere from 6 to 16 frames for good results. There are times, however, when it can last longer. I usually start out by designing the final look or a lightning bolt that I'm happy with for the particular shot I will be working on (see Figure 17.1).

From there I work backward. I eliminate parts of the bolt (1) design by keeping track of key areas of the bolt as I go along to use for my final animation (see Figure 17.2).

I then reverse the process and start "flipping" as I start to animate forward. I animate using the previously broken-down keys (5 through 1), adding trailing bolts if I animate (snap) the main bolt to another position (1 to 2). These dissipate in two to three frames, and I trace back the main bolt's previous position (residual). I trace this "residual" image more thinly

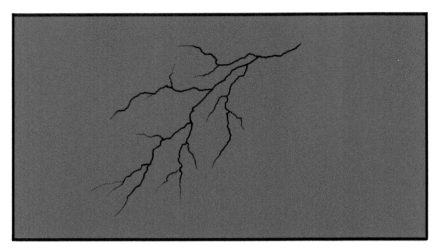

FIG 17.1 Breakdown lightning design 1.

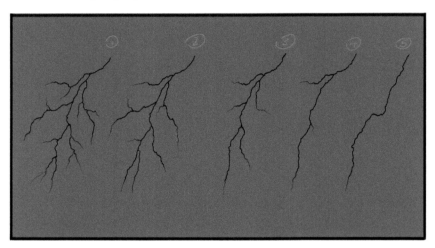

FIG 17.2 Breakdown lightning design 2.

with each succeeding frame. At this point, I illustrate the images in white, because when you animate for production you will be drawing in black graphite or ink and these images are then reversed when being composited (see Figure 17.3).

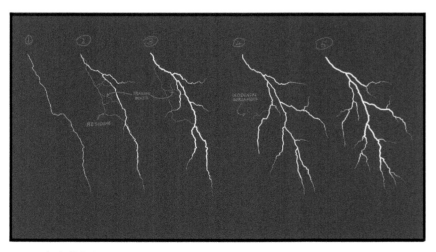

FIG 17.3 Look of lightning in negative.

The trace back can be as few as 3 or as many as 16 frames (see Figure 17.4).

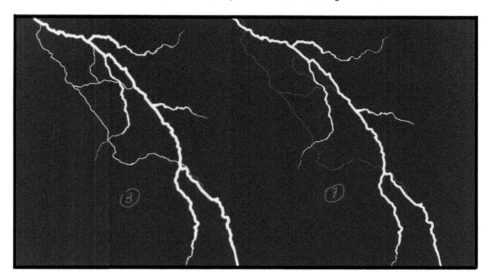

FIG 17.4 Traceback of residual image.

I will also add some incidental fine streamers lasting two to four frames (these need only be trace-back images). The final animation of the bolt does not necessarily have to look like your initial design. That was just a placeholder to help guide your animation, not something that needed to be adhered to (see Figure 17.5). (Remember: Don't fall in love with your drawings!)

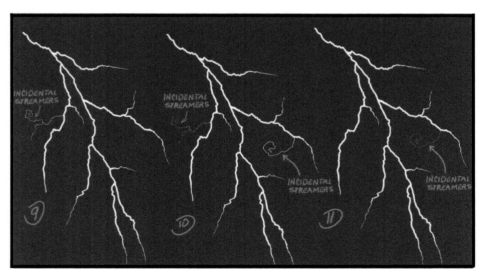

FIG 17.5 Adding incidental streamers.

In order to get good lines that will read well, I use a variety of pencils. I may start with an H (hard) lead pencil for my fine lines up to a 9B (soft) for the thicker lines and to get a good black line. Adding color is another option when assembling all your lightning elements for final composite (see Figure 17.6).

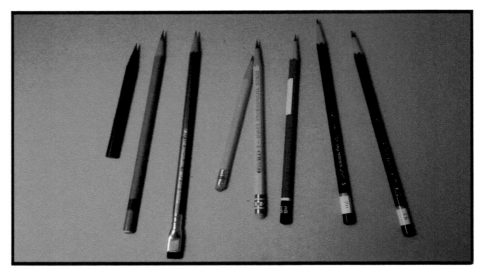

FIG 17.6 Pencil variety.

Make sure that the bolt is always moving downward. Use some points of the jaggedness on the bolt as markers that you can follow in your animation that will clearly show directional movement. You can label them as numbers, letters, or just plain hash marks (see Figure 17.7).

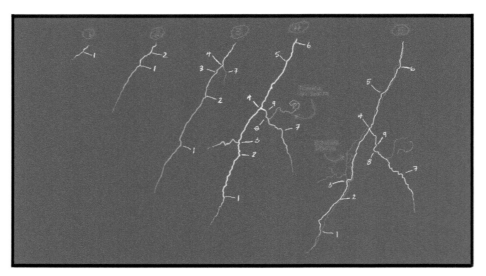

FIG 17.7 Mark off points on the bolt to track movement.

Electricity follows the same principles as lightning but with a gentler, meandering rhythm. The snapping of the electric bolts is a bit more lively and prolonged as it works its way between conductors, a steady stream of current that wraps around an object, enveloping it in its charge (see Figure 17.8).

Electricity, once drawn to a conductive surface, will wrap around it. The current works its way over the contours of that object (see Figure 17.9).

The electric bolts leave residual images of themselves as they snap to new positions around the object, even as newer currents of electricity snake over it (see Figure 17.10).

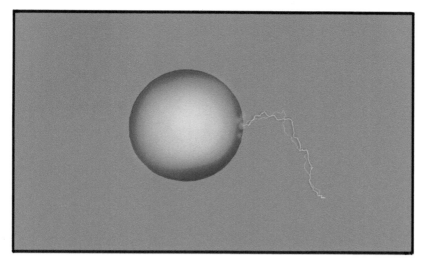

FIG 17.8 Electricity animation.

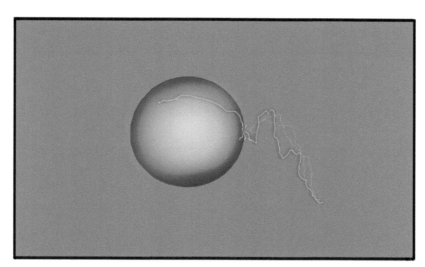

FIG 17.9 Bolt wraps round the contours.

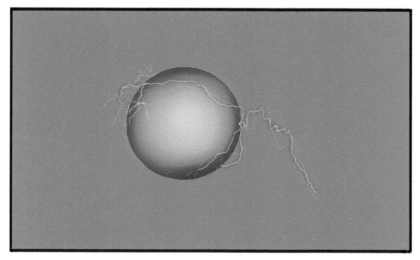

FIG 17.10 Bolt snakes over the surface.

Both new and older bolts flow over the surface, dancing over it and emitting finer tendrils from their encompassing fingers (see Figure 17.11).

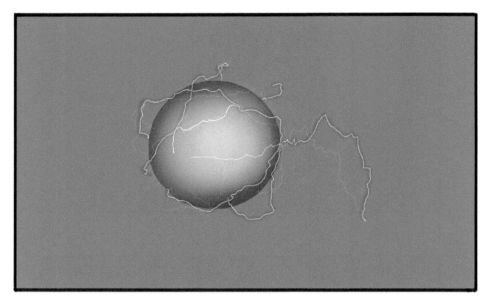

FIG 17.11 Bolt constantly flows over surface.

The current will continue to cover the object, moving up, down, and around it until the source is shut down (see Figure 17.12).

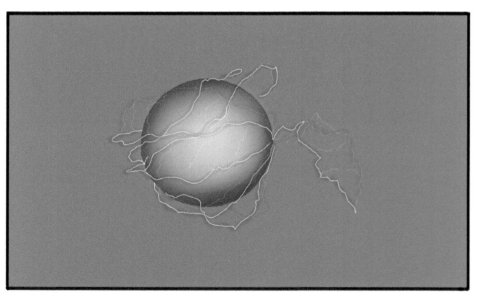

FIG 17.12 Electricity dances off the surface.

Jacob's ladder is a term that describes an electric charge that "climbs" up two conducting rods like someone stepping up a ladder one step at a time (see Figure 17.13).

The steps are made with residual images trailing behind the main bolt (see Figures 17.14 and 17.15).

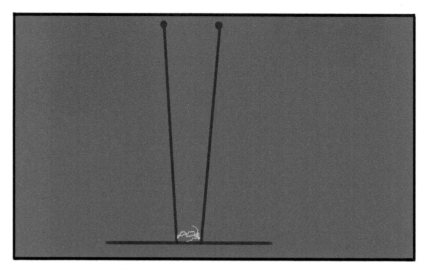

FIG 17.13 Residual images trail behind main bolt.

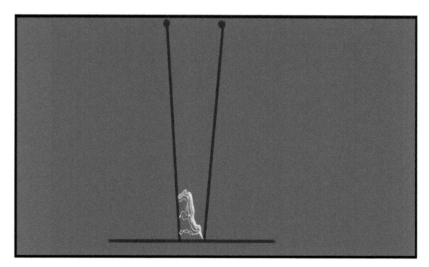

FIG 17.14 Bolt snaps upward.

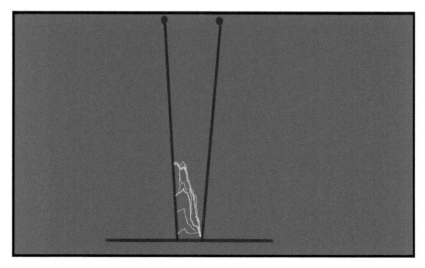

FIG 17.15 Residuals trail behind.

The residual images act like speed lines, giving impetus to the upward movement (see Figures 17.16 through 17.21).

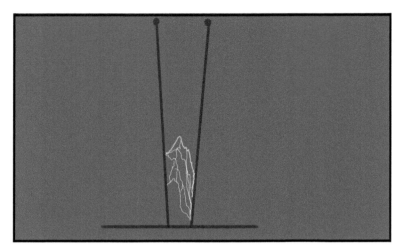

FIG 17.16 Residuals mimic speed lines.

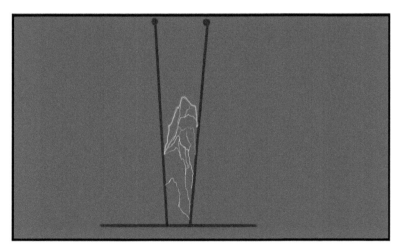

FIG 17.17 Bolt is deliberate in its upward climb.

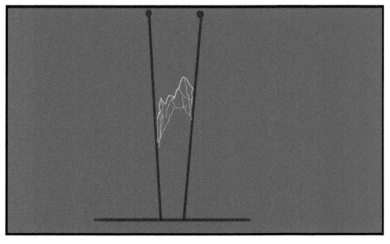

FIG 17.18 Bolt make back and forth action.

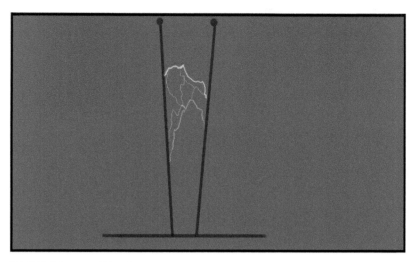

FIG 17.19 Bolt moves quickly to the top.

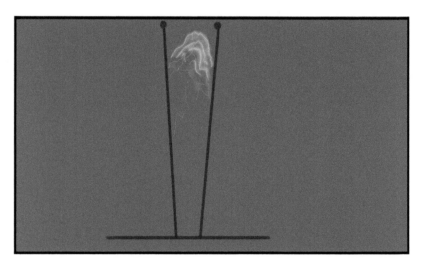

FIG 17.20 Starts to fade on its last leg.

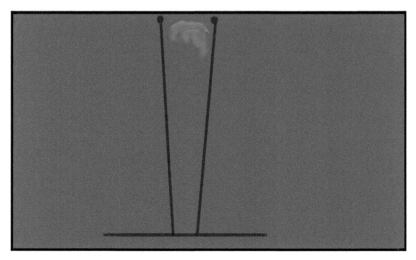

FIG 17.21 Fades off.

What follows is the method to trace back the image of a previous frame (residual) when the bolt changes or snaps into another position. The trailing tendrils act to link the abrupt change in direction. The trace-back of the images or residual images can last for as few as three frames and as many as 16 frames. This is something that animators must judge for themselves, taking into account the intent of the effect. The tendril images should not last for more than three to five frames. Always keep the animation of the bolt moving forward (see Figure 17.22).

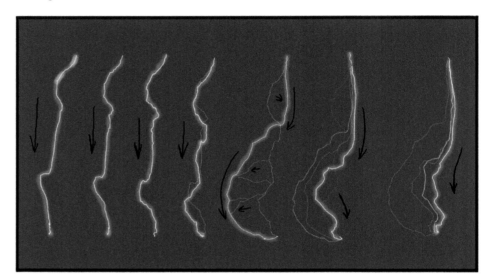

FIG 17.22 Traced back images.

CHAPTER 18

Explosions

*Although personally I am content with existing explosives,
I feel we must not stand in the path of improvement.*

—*Winston Churchill*

Most explosions are a combination of fireball and smoke and debris. Rather than using just smoke and dust and debris, you may want to add a color element like fire mixed in with the smoke. Recreating these dramatic type of explosions in traditional effects animation takes a multitude of layered elements. So let's try out a few examples that we can animate.

Let's start with three levels for our first explosion example. To begin with, I'll animate the line drawing from start to finish. My second level will be the smoke level, and then the third will be the fiery interior of the blast (see Figures 18.1 and 18.2).

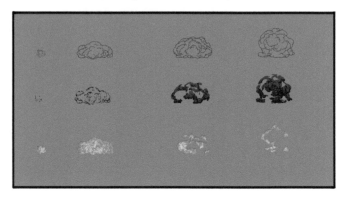

FIG 18.1 Separate levels of an explosion 1.

FIG **18.2** Separate levels of an explosion 2.

Before all three elements are sandwiched together, however, you will need to treat each separately, so that when they are composited they will blend seamlessly as one unit. By blurring and diffusing each a little and by enhancing the intensity of the color values, you can boost and magnify the effect (see Figure 18.3).

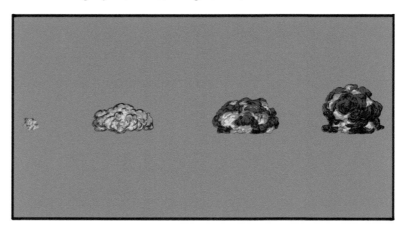

FIG **18.3** Combine three elements.

The fire level will diminish as the explosion progresses, leaving mostly smoke and debris to culminate the effect (see Figure 18.4).

FIG **18.4** Firey element fades within.

An explosion that occurs in the air will discharge and expand in all directions, given that there are no obstructions to deflect the detonation. Small pieces of debris may be expelled and fly off faster than the explosion expands (see Figures 18.5 and 18.6).

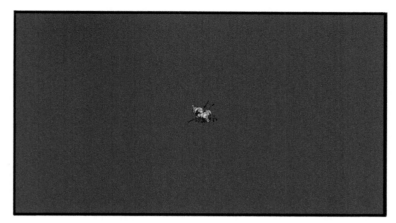

FIG 18.5 In-air explosion.

FIG 18.6 Explosion expands in all directions.

This type of explosion can be animated in a minimum of two levels—one for the fireball level and another, darker level to give the explosion a more dimensional look and feel (1 and 2) (see Figure 18.7).

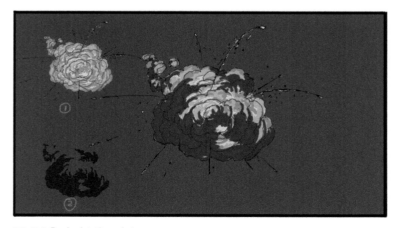

FIG 18.7 Two levels in the explosion.

The inferno expands quickly and once it reaches its maximum radius will dissipate at a much slower rate. Don't forget to indicate some of the elements of the explosion on the far side of the effect to get a sense of dimensionality to it. This can be done simply by animating a separate level that is darker and mirrors the top level of animation, diminishing in size away from the camera, while exposing it under the top level of the explosion animation (see Figures 18.8 and 18.9).

FIG 18.8 Maximum expansion.

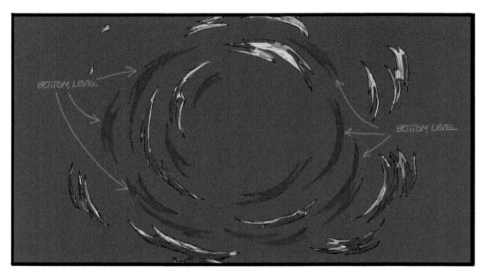

FIG 18.9 Elements dissipate.

A bomb explosion on the ground can only explode away from its detonation point, up and away, and expand or radiate from that point along the ground plane. Here, again, it is wise to be aware of the ground plane so you can animate to the proper perspective as the explosion expands along that ground plane. Leading the expansion of the explosion is a shock-wave element that's traveling at a faster rate.

Sparks and flying debris shoot out from the center as the smoke level rolls outward from the impact point (see Figures 18.10 through 18.12).

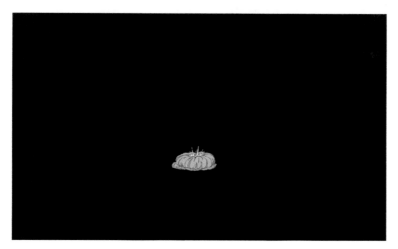

FIG 18.10 Flat ground explosion.

FIG 18.11 Explodes up and out.

FIG 18.12 Firey trials stark away from center.

Even if the explosion tends to favor one side over the rest, it will expand primarily upward (see Figures 18.13 and 18.14).

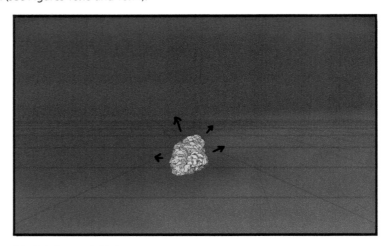

FIG **18.13** Asymmetrical design.

FIG **18.14** Up, out, and away from center.

Once the initial blast rockets upward, the debris and smoke will start expanding outward as well (see Figures 18.15 and 18.16).

FIG **18.15** Adding debris.

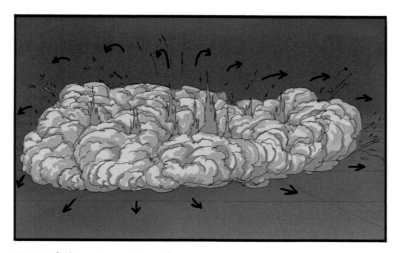

FIG 18.16 Quick expansion to maximum radius.

Keep the smoke rolling away from the impact point. Keep the shapes rounded and irregular, as well as varying in size; try to stay away from similar shapes and twinning (see Figure 18.17).

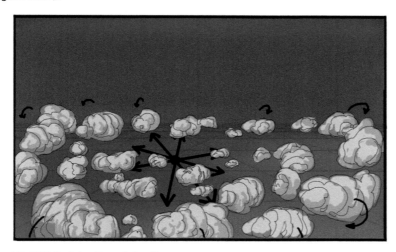

FIG 18.17 Smoke breaking up/fading off.

CHAPTER 19

Fire Hoses and Faucets

My books are like water; those of great geniuses are like wine.
(Fortunately) everybody drinks water.

—*Mark Twain*

Water coming out of a fire hose can only go as far as the pressure under which it is being pumped. Fire trucks provide the pressure through the use of their pumps so it can travel great distances to extinguish fires not easily reached because of the tremendous heat. (Great respect for fire fighters everywhere!)

The nozzle of a fire hose controls the stream, from a steady and powerful torrent that will reach distant fires to a wide spray that quenches smoldering ones (see Figures 19.1 and 19.2).

FIG 19.1 Fire hose stream start to finish.

FIG 19.2 Various types of stream.

Without pumps, whether they were hand-operated pumps or today's electric high-pressure pumps, to generate the pressure to force the water out of the hose in a flash and with great force, the water would trickle out like the water in a garden hose (see Figure 19.3).

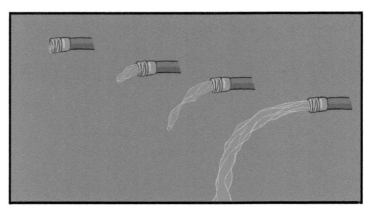

FIG 19.3 Garden hose water.

The water will come out of the hose streamlined (1 and 2), taking on the shape of the round-shaped hose, but then the water will start to turn turbulent as it travels through the air (3). The weight of it makes it arc gracefully to the ground (4) (see Figure 19.4).

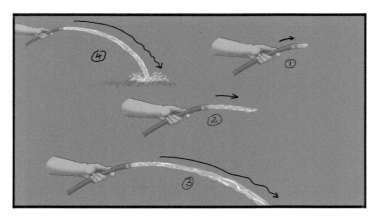

FIG 19.4 Garden hose stream progression.

If you employ a tool with a garden hose, such as a nozzle that constrains and minimizes the opening through which the water emerges, the water builds up pressure behind that nozzle. When it eventually does exit through the smaller opening, it shoots out at a greater velocity and is cone-shaped (1). It fans out and eventually forms a smaller, more compact stream (4) that can travel a greater distance with greater force. When the nozzle is restricted and closed off, the water eases off and spreads with diminished force as it stops (5) (see Figure 19.5).

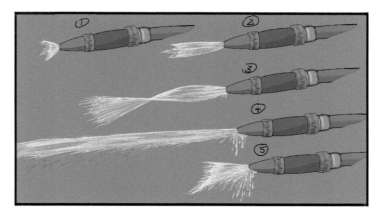

FIG 19.5 Garden hose with a nozzle.

When water pours out of a faucet, it too comes out in a streamlined form due to the shape of the pipe (1–3) but then turns turbulent because of air friction and diminished constriction after it leaves the round pipe (4). Aerators on the faucet stabilize the turbulence and make the flow of water out of the faucet more streamlined and uniform (5) (see Figure 19.6).

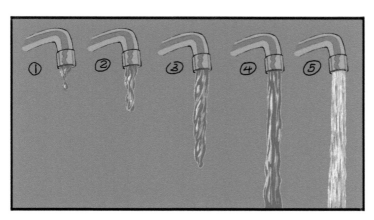

FIG 19.6 Indoor faucet stream.

CHAPTER 20

Straight Ahead and Pose to Pose

March on. Do not tarry. To go forward is to move toward perfection.

—*Kahlil Gibran*

Straight-ahead animation is the practice of animating a character or an effects element in a chronological progression of events—in other words, animating the element from start to finish from Frame 1 to its conclusion. In effects animation, this method is most effective and practical when used on elements such as fire, pixie dust, or water splashes. It's a more instinctual process wherein the flow of the animation takes on a more organic and spontaneous quality rather than having a stiff or unnatural slant to it. Fire is the best example of this technique. Fire moves in a chaotic fashion, erratic in its turmoil and action, and therefore it is best to animate it without the need for preset poses to follow. Here I've animated a sequence of fire drawings on twos. I animated it straight ahead in rough stage (see Figure 20.1).

The fire is not a realistic fire design and has a bit of an edgier look but will still move like regular fire when it's cleaned up. Working straight ahead allows me the freedom to be capricious in how I handle the tongues of fire shooting off the ends of the flames so they can dart off haphazardly (see Figure 20.2 through 20.4).

Pose to pose is a more planned and controlled process of animating. Using key poses as guidelines for the animation, you can plan your action and timing out from start to finish. Be careful, however, that those poses don't compromise your final animation! The idea here is to use the poses as guidelines, not as concrete "must hit" poses. They are something to aim for, but allow yourself some play here where you may need to alter your animation and/or your timing. Think of it as a road map for your action—there may be shortcuts or more scenic routes along the way. So give yourself permission to change the animation in a

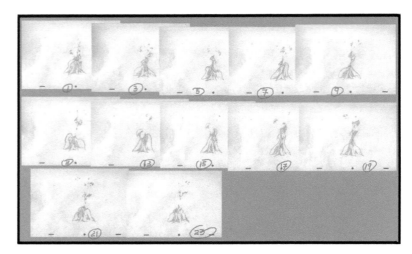

FIG 20.1 Rough straight-ahead animation.

FIG 20.2 Straight ahead animation.

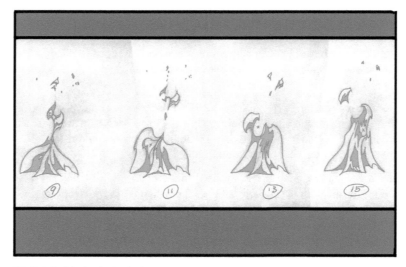

FIG 20.3 Straight ahead animation 1.

FIG 20.4 Straight ahead animation 2.

direction that may feel better as you move forward. Remember, you don't want to fall in love with your drawings to the point that your animation is muddled (see Figure 20.5).

FIG 20.5 Pose-to-pose animation.

Pose to pose also allows you to animate your action, leaving breakdowns and inbetweens that your follow-up assistant can fill in as you move on to other elements in your shot. You need to make clear and concise timing charts for the assistant to easily interpret, thus speeding up the process (see Figure 20.6).

Give indications of arcs to follow or any registration marks that may be necessary so the assistant knows just how much of the element needs to be drawn and the proper placement of it against the background. Indicate the proper spacing of the drawings on the charts to make it absolutely clear (see Figures 20.7 and 20.8).

Go as far as to write down the spacing indications: whether they are to be spaced one-half the distance between your extremes or a third of the way; if you want the drawings to

FIG 20.6 Pose to pose animation with chart.

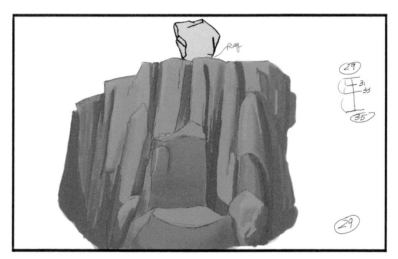

FIG 20.7 Back and forth action.

FIG 20.8 Register rock to background.

favor one extreme over the other to indicate a slow out of one extreme to the other or a slow into your next extreme. You can never give too much information to help your follow-up artists (see Figure 20.9).

FIG 20.9 Be specific with instructions on timing.

Rough out a breakdown drawing for tricky timing to be absolutely clear about spacing or arc directions to be sure you get what you want (see Figure 20.10). When no inbetweens are necessary, simply don't have a chart (see Figure: 20.11).

The effects animator is responsible for drawing all the key drawings of any of the effects elements in a scene. If the element changes direction, mass, or dimensions of any kind, such as the rock splitting in this case, the animator needs to draw all of the drawings that show the progression of the change. This would be true even if it required that the animator do all

FIG 20.10 Rough out the animation.

FIG 20.11 Pose out animated keys.

of them in sequential order or every other drawing to ease the burden of guesswork on the follow-up assistants (see Figures 20.12 and 20.13).

FIG 20.12 Follow through all details.

Assistants are responsible for bringing any inconsistencies that they may encounter to the attention of the animator. The animator may have meant to do what the assistant perceives as a mistake, but the responsible thing for the assistant to do would be to clarify either through a phone call or a visit to the animator's office to meet with the animator directly. (The best option!) But the responsibility is always on the animator to make sure everything is clearly defined. Never assume one person or the other is correct! This way, the assistant will learn something new from the incorrect assumption of a mistake, or the animator will learn to trust and gain more confidence in the assistant. Either way, the checks and balances in this type of collaborative association will make for a smoother running production.

Rough animation of an effects prop is sufficient if there exists a model sheet of the element, especially if the animator and assistant have worked with each together before and have a

FIG 20.13 Animate details through to the end.

good working relationship. An experienced animator knows how much he or she needs to leave for the assistant to complete the scene. An experienced animator also does not take for granted that the assistant following up his or her work will know what the animator's intentions were instinctively but will make certain that the animation is thoroughly worked out before leaving his or her hands. Scenes don't always go to the same assistant. Very often the scenes are distributed into the assistant pool as the assistants become available, so an animator doesn't always work with the same person. Throughout the production, the pool of animators and the pool of assistants become acquainted with each other's working styles, as everyone works back and forth with a variety of artists and there ends up being a harmonious synergy and mutual trust as people work together more and more. Early on in my career, one of my old mentors, Volus Jones, once told me, "Assume that the assistant that follows you up doesn't know anything! That will keep you on your toes!"

The system of animator to assistant to inbetweener is set up not only to allow the animator to work faster and speed up the production process but also to allow training for the follow-up artists, whether assistants or inbetweeners. Collaboration between all disciplines is the strongest guarantee that the production will keep moving forward in a timely and efficient manner.

CHAPTER 21

Bouncing Ball

Our greatest glory is not in never falling, but in rising every time we fall.

—Confucius

A great way to learn and practice timing is the bouncing ball routine. We will use several different objects in this exercise. How do I approach animating these objects? I need to consider the mass of each object, and the flexibility of its shell, its texture, and composition will also give me some insight. But my best reflection and study will be the fact that I've already seen these objects in action and witnessed them over my lifetime and know how these objects have reacted. So I have experience stored in my memories. I just need to recall what I already know and use these memories plus a little imagination and caricaturization to help me animate them.

Let's think about the science of it first! The energy of motion, or *kinetic energy*, the energy an object builds up as it's falling from a table, deforms the object (squash) and converts it to *potential energy* when it hits the floor. That potential energy now gives the object its ability to bounce back up. This potential energy, or stored-up energy, as it is squashing enables the object to now transfer or release that energy to return to its original shape by discharging it (stretch). The amount of "bounce" an object has depends on its composition: hardness, surface texture, size, its core makeup, and so on. These are all mental exercises I would like you to ponder as you work out the possibilities.

A beach ball is very light, with hardly any weight or mass associated with it. It therefore can't build up a lot of energy as it falls. Its shell is very flexible and it doesn't have a core density, other than the fact that it's full of air. So unless propelled by someone hitting it, it won't bounce very much. The timing charts will show us how fast it slows down during its squash and springs upward in the recoil and where it will slow down at the apex of its arc as it bounces up and down. In this example, it takes the beach ball seven frames to roll off the table and touch the ground. From Frames 1 to 6, the ball builds energy by moving faster. Note the spacing on the timing chart. On Frame 7, it touches the ground but doesn't squash yet (see Figure 21.1).

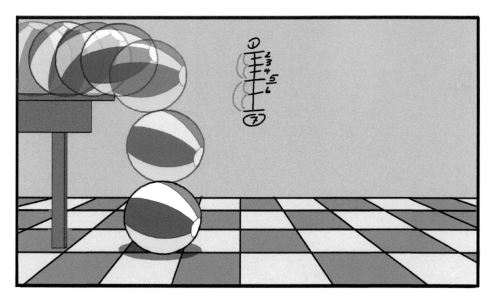

FIG 21.1 Beach ball bounce.

On Frame 8 the ball squashes, building potential energy. It then releases it, bouncing upward (Frame 10; stretch), regaining its shape (Frame 11), then slowing into its next key pose (Frame 15) as it reaches its maximum height. Again, note the timing chart (see Figure 21.2).

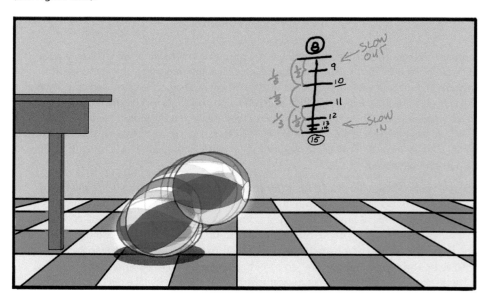

FIG 21.2 Squash and stretch.

Because the beach ball doesn't have the mass to build up a lot of energy, it lacks the force behind the bounce to rebound as high as the height from which it was dropped. So it will only bounce so high (Frame 15) before gravity forces it to arc back to the ground again (Frame 20) (see Figure 21.3).

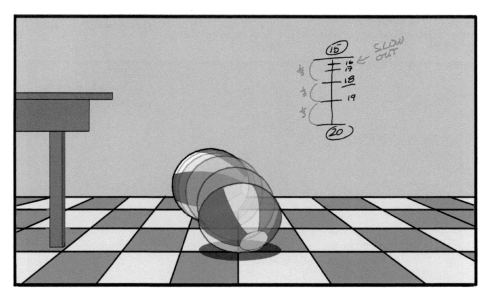

FIG 21.3 Ball arcs back to ground.

A tennis ball has a thick rubber shell covered in a felt-like material and filled with pressurized air, made for maximum bounce specifications. Once it hits the ground its potential energy (squash) is released rapidly into another bounce (stretch) due to its composition of rubber shell and pressurized air designed specifically to make it bounce. When it reaches the apex of its bounce, it slows (slow in) as gravity starts pulling at it, and it arcs back down (slow out), speeding up on its descent (see Figure 21.4).

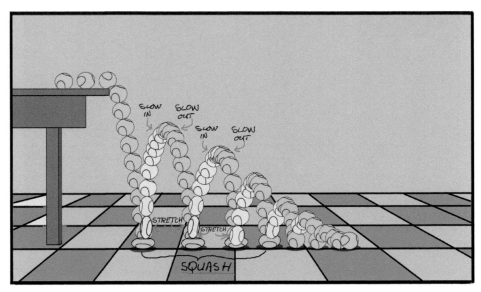

FIG 21.4 Tennis ball bounce.

A baseball has a rubber-coated cork core covered with tightly woven woolen and polyester yarn that is in turn covered in rubber cement and a shell of cowhide tightly stitched over all. It's made to bounce when hit by a baseball bat. When dropped, it will not build up the same kinetic energy as when thrown by a pitcher, and therefore it won't have the chance to build the potential energy that is produced by a bat hitting it. Note that the baseball doesn't bounce as high as the tennis ball. In addition, the baseball doesn't bounce as many times because of its lack of potential energy—because it disburses that energy into its own mass rather than releasing it as the tennis ball does (see Figure 21.5).

FIG 21.5 Baseball bounce.

A bowling ball has a very dense mass and is heavy (see Figure 21.6).

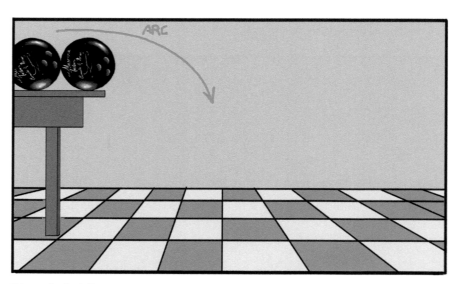

FIG 21.6 Bowling ball bounce.

As heavy as it is, it will follow a smooth arc as it falls even though its weight could topple the table (see Figures 21.7 through 21.9).

FIG 21.7 Heavy ball topples table.

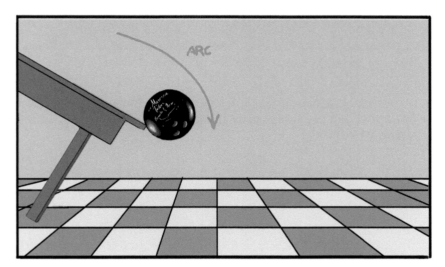

FIG 21.8 Ball follows arc as it falls.

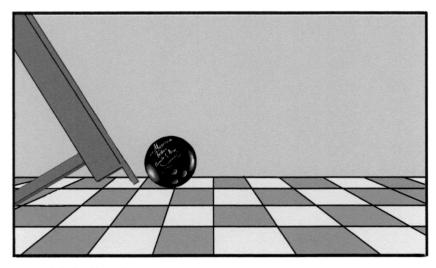

FIG 21.9 Ball strike with great force.

The potential energy is almost all distributed into itself because of its great, dense mass (see Figures 21.10).

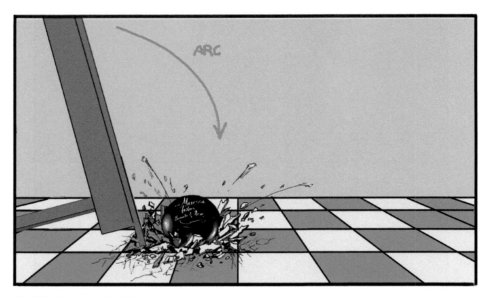

FIG 21.10 Heavy dense object little to no bounce.

So the lessons we learned here are that, no matter the weight or composition, an object will always follow an arc as it travels through the air and, of course, never ever drop a bowling ball on a ceramic tiled floor!

CHAPTER 22

Exposure Sheets

Yield not to calamity, but face her boldly.

—Virgil

The exposure sheet of an animation project is a source of order in a production where collaboration is the essential key to wrangling a multitude of divergent subdivisions and collecting them for one prodigious outcome. Or as someone once said, "It's a train wreck in slow motion!" The *exposure sheet*, or X-sheet, is a document that's always included in and follows each scene folder in an animated production from one department to the next at each production stage. It lists what each department does in each scene. The layout of an X-sheet is set up this way. The top of the page has a horizontal strip with an area specified for a production number in the top left corner. Next, to the right of this is a space for a sequence number, a scene number, the names of artists who will animate on the scene, and finally the length of the scene and the page number (see Figure 22.1).

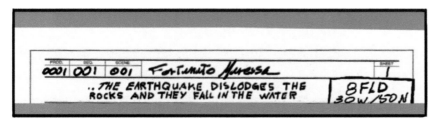

FIG 22.1 The exposure sheet.

The majority of the sheet is a series of vertical columns and horizontal delineations denoting the frame counts of the scene. The vertical columns represent the different levels of artwork necessary for the scene. At the far left appears a wide column labeled *Action*. Here, the director or animator can make timing notes or thumbnails to further define the action that takes place in the scene. To the right of this level is the dialogue track level. This is where the sound editor will break down the voice-over dialogue or any sound effects taking place in the scene (see Figure 22.2).

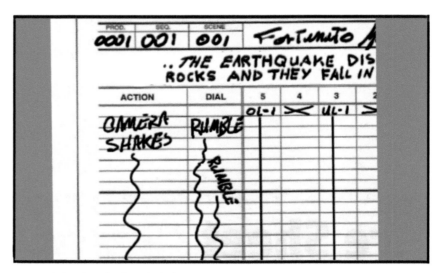

FIG 22.2 Action column describes action in shot.

At the far right appears a column for instructions to the camera department (see Figure 22.3).

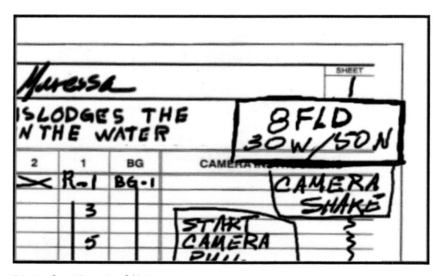

FIG 22.3 Camera instructions, field size.

The layout department is responsible for setting up the scene. They will indicate the proper format in which the camera will shoot the scene. If there is a camera move within the shot, they will indicate this according to a standard set grid that the cameraman will be able to adhere to. If a camera pan occurs in the scene, how fast it will be and where it will start and stop will be indicated, trucking in and out from a close-up to a long shot, camera tilts, and so on (see Figure 22.4).

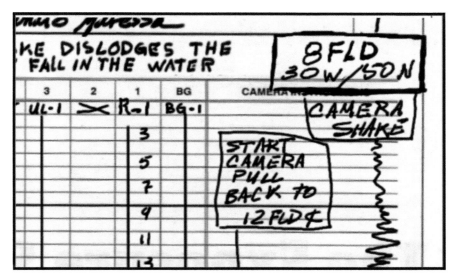

FIG 22.4 Camera moves, pans, and trucks.

A 16-field chart would be the standard maximum size of the overall picture frame used within this particular production (see Figure 22.5).

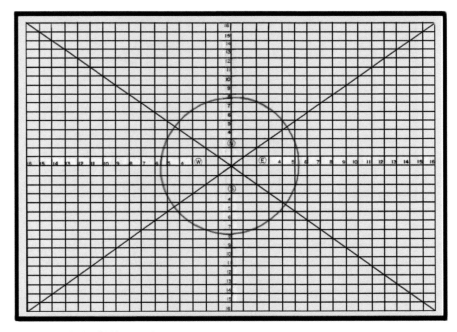

FIG 22.5 Standard 16-field format grid.

The instructions, worded *8 fld* (field), *30W/50N*, mean that the camera would be set to an eight-field framing within a *16-field chart*. *30W* (west)/*50N* (north) are specific start positions. Pull back to a *12 fld Center*, which would be the stop positions within the overall picture frame (see Figure 22.6).

Cross dissolves and the use of opacity and diffusion filters. If for some reason there are levels that switch position at any point, instructions for that would also be written in this column. This would be for the animation check department because of any registration problems that may occur that would be checked and noted down the line (see Figure 22.7).

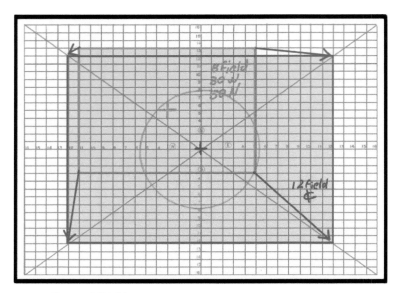

FIG 22.6 Charting a field shift/move.

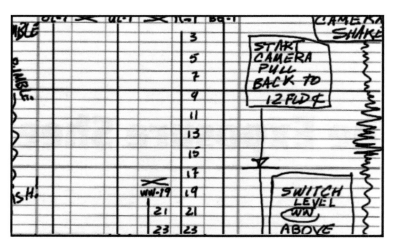

FIG 22.7 Exposure levels of elements.

All the levels between the dialogue and camera instruction are for the different art, the background, the overlays (OL) and underlays (UL), and of course the character and effects animation. The bottom most level is on the far right; this would usually be the painted background (BG), while the topmost would be on the far left (see Figure 22.8).

Here's a breakdown of the levels and how they stack together bottom to top (see Figure 22.9).

The OL and UL are layout levels in the scene that are painted but may lay on top of the background with character or effects levels in between. A UL may be exposed sandwiched between an OL and animated elements, the UL and more animated elements, and the BG (see Figure 22.10).

All information compiled on an X-sheet will help organize the work as it travels through the production pipeline, helping all the departments down the line understand the history of a scene from start to finish and to maintain the history and continuity. It would then be stored along with the scene, in addition to the animation and layout artwork. This could then be used by future animation filmmakers for reference so that similar techniques may be used in future projects, as is often done.

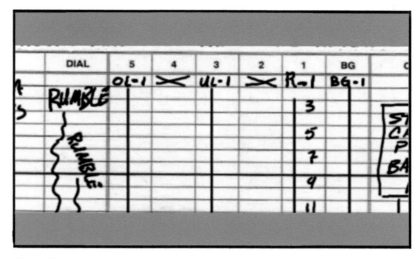

FIG 22.8 Exposing elements on columns.

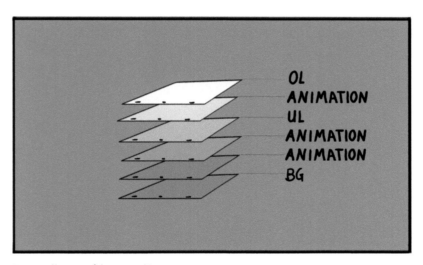

FIG 22.9 Placement of elements stacking.

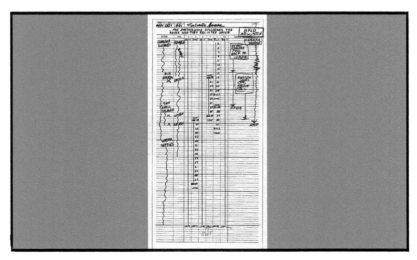

FIG 22.10 Simple completed exposure sheet.

Index